PATTERNS OF CONTACT WITH RELATIVES

by

Sheila R. Klatzky

Department of Sociology
University of Wisconsin

THE ARNOLD AND CAROLINE ROSE
MONOGRAPH SERIES IN SOCIOLOGY

A gift by Arnold and Caroline Rose to the American Sociological Association in 1968 provided for the establishment of the Arnold and Caroline Rose Monograph Series in Sociology. The conveyance provided for the publication of manuscripts in any subject matter field of sociology. The donors intended the series for rather short monographs, contributions that normally are beyond the scope of publication in regular academic journals.

The Series is under the general direction of an editorial board appointed by the Council of the American Sociological Association and responsible to the Publications Committee of the Association. Competition for publication in the Series has been limited by the Association to Fellow, Active and Student members.

Library of Congress Number 71-183125
International Standard Book Number 0-912764-06-6

© American Sociological Association
1722 N St. N.W.
Washington, D.C. 20036

TABLE OF CONTENTS

LIST OF TABLES AND FIGURES

PREFACE

The research literature on behavior toward kin in Western industrialized societies, while rich in insightful descriptions of diverse local areas, still lacks in quantitative testing of the hypotheses these studies suggest. What quantitative work does exist is of limited usefulness not only because of the nature of the techniques but also because the samples in many cases are representative either of no known population, or of populations of very limited composition.

The present study also has its shortcomings. In the first place, its subject matter is confined to variation in the frequency with which male members of a national random sample contact their male relatives, including father, oldest brother, male cousin, brother-in-law, and maternal and paternal grandfathers and uncles. Moreover, the data were gathered over a short period of time, so that hypotheses about longitudinal change in the nature of family contact could not be tested. Furthermore, there are no tests of hypotheses about attitudinal variables such as affection or congeniality. Explanatory variables are limited to distance, occupational status and mobility, religion, ethnicity, size of city, region, and the location and frequency of contacts with relatives other than the one in question. The two last-named variables are used in studying the interdependence of contacts with various relatives.

Some readers may not be familiar with all of the research techniques used here. They include regression, multiple classification analysis, and path analysis. I have relegated to appendices technical material not directly essential for comprehension and what could not be disposed of in this fashion I tried to make as intelligible as possible in the text. A summary of the major findings is included in the last chapter to aid readers in wading through the technical details on which the findings are based.

ACKNOWLEDGEMENTS

This monograph is based on my doctoral dissertation, submitted at the University of Chicago. I wish to express my thanks to my dissertation chairman, Professor Robert W. Hodge, who made the data available, advised me in the preliminary analysis, and was extremely helpful in correspondence on the completed chapters. Professor Hodge also recommended that I use the research training fellowship generously provided me by the Social Science Research Council for the 1969-1970 academic year to study and do research under the direction of Professor Otis Dudley Duncan at the University of Michigan. Professor Duncan, who agreed to serve as acting chairman of my dissertation, not only gave me generously of his time and ideas, but also set before me an example of social science at its best.

I am also grateful to the Social Science Research Council, which provided me with the opportunity to receive research training I would not otherwise have received; to the Population Studies Center at the University of Michigan for granting me the use of its facilities during my year in residence; to J. Michael Coble, who patiently and ingeniously helped me in solving problems of programming and data processing; to the Sociology Department of the University of Michigan, which provided me with computer time for directed research; and to the unnamed reviewers who read this manuscript and offered suggestions for its improvement.

Last, but not least, I wish to thank the members of my family, who provided me with living exhibits of hypotheses to be tested.

None of those mentioned is responsible for the errors in this document. While they deserve much of the credit for its virtue, I assume all of the blame for its faults.

CHAPTER 1

RESIDENTIAL PROPINQUITY
AND PARENTAL CONTACT

Introduction

Residential propinquity has long been recognized as a powerful force affecting the frequency of various kinds of social interaction. As early as 1932, for example, Bossard found that of 5,000 marriages in which one or both applicants for the license were residents of Philadelphia, the percentage of marriages decreased as distance between residences (measured in number of blocks) increased. The frequency of contact between kin, the form of social interaction studied in the present research, is no less subject to the influence of distance. However, the form and the extent of that influence have not yet been established. As most students of family structure, kinship, and related subjects know, there has been extensive disagreement about the effect of industrialization on the strength of family ties. One position, taken by Parsons (1954) and others is that the occupational system in an industrialized society demands a high degree of geographical mobility which, combined with the necessity of treating people in the occupational system as individuals rather than members of ascriptive kinship units, entails the curtailment of extended family encounters.[1]

This argument, however, contains at least three causal links—each of which may or may not be independent of the others. Basically, it claims that industrialization increases the distance between residences of kinfolk; that increased distance (as well as other factors) decreases the frequency of contact between them; and that the less frequent face-to-face contact weakens other family ties besides those requiring face-to-face contact.

The major source of disagreement with this position is the assumption that face-to-face contact is necessary to maintain family ties, providing the latter are not defined by the former (for example, Litwak, 1960; Litwak and Szelenyi, 1969; and Sussman and Burchinal, 1962). Others have taken issue with the assumption that kin groups are widely dispersed in industrialized societies, pointing to the extensiveness of kinship networks in various local areas. (See, for example, Sussman, 1959). The existence of extensive kinship networks in particular local areas does not, of course, refute the hypothesis that industrialization has led to wider dispersion of kinfolk over time.

The second causal link — that between distance and frequency of kin contact — has apparently been overlooked because it seemed so obvious. In some studies frequency of kin contact is reported only of those whose kin live in the same local area as the respondent. If the sample is thus made homogeneous with respect to distance, then, of course, the effect of variation in distance cannot be measured. Even in these studies, however, there is till the possibility that variation in residential distance within local areas may be affecting frequency of contact. As long as distance is independent of the other variables assumed to affect kin contact, this would not affect estimates of the effects of the other variables. However, if the other variables are correlated with distance, then their apparent effects may be simply the effect of distance. If, for example, people of lower socioeconomic status are likely to live closer to their relatives, then the finding that people of lower socioeconomic status visit relatives more frequently may be due simply to differences in propinquity.[2] It thus becomes important to establish as accurately as possible the effect of distance between residences on frequency of contact.

Alternative Models

The studies which have explicitly included distance as a variable have considered it either as dichotomous or as a set of categories (for example, Reiss, 1962; Adams, 1968; Stuckert, 1963; Litwak, 1960). They show that kin contact is a monotonically decreasing function of distance — that is, the frequency of contact declines steadily as distance increases. This seems reasonable, since we do not expect contact to increase with an increase in distance anywhere in the given range. In addition, at least one study indicates that the importance of distance may vary in different ranges. In regard to interaction with parents, Adams remarks (1968: pp. 37-39):

It almost seems that living in the same city with one's parents makes frequent interaction imperative, living over 100 miles apart makes frequent interaction impossible, while living in different communities but within 100 miles leaves room for a modicum of personal choice.

This argument suggests that while the expected (or mean) frequency of contact declines continuously with distance, its variation around the expected value in a given range of distance will be greatest in people living outside the city but within 100 miles of their parents. This hypothesis (which will be examined later in relation to the present data) is mentioned in order to point out that in order to test hypotheses about the variation in contact at given expected frequencies of contact it is first necessary to assume an underlying model to generate the expected frequency of contact at different distances. Different models will provide different predicted contact frequencies and will make different assumptions about the nature of the interaction. The use of categories, for example, suggests that the effect of distance may be nonmonotonic. Since we have little reason to believe that as between any two distance values, people are on the average likely to visit more frequently at the greater distance, it seems sensible to assume that kin contact is a monotonic function of distance. Furthermore, since we have no reason to think that there are inherent breaks or discontinuities in the distance-contact relationship, it seems reasonable to assume that frequency of kin contact is a continuous as well as a montonic function of distance.

On the assumptions of continuity and monotonicity, and in the absence of information about the actual process underlying the relationship between two variables, the usual procedure is to assume a linear relationship and to use linear regression techniques to estimate its parameters. $C_i = b_0 + b_1 D_i + e_i$ (where C_i = contacts per year; D_i = distance in miles; and e_i is an error term specific to the ith individual) would be such a model. However, a linear model implies that the slope (measured by b_1 in this model) or the expected amount of change in the dependent variable in response to a change in the independent variable is constant, regardless of the value of the latter. In the present case, this means that the expected increase in kin contact, following upon a given decrease in distance, will be the same regardless of which part of the distance range we are talking about and regardless of the frequency of contact. The costs involved in making one additional visit (for example, changing from one to two contacts per year) when one lives 1,000 miles away, are obviously much greater than the costs involved in making one additional visit when one lives next door or down the block. Yet the increment in visiting is the same in each case. If distance is considered as an indicator of these costs, then this argument implies that the effect of distance will differ at different distances. In such a case a linear model is inappropriate.

The argument can be stated more formally by saying that the *change* we expect in contact frequency following a given change in distance depends on, or is a function of, the distance. Here again one must decide what kind of function to assume. If we suppose that this rate of change is a continuous and monotonic function of distance, then the simplest model is one which assumes that the rate of change in frequency of contact accompanying a given change in distance is proprtional to distance or to a monotonic function of distance. Here again, in the absence of specific knowledge about the process by which the rate of change in contact with kin is related to distance, we can only start with the simplest model and see how well or how badly it describes our data. This model can be written:

Equation 1, $C_i = b_0 D_i^{b_1}$ where C_i = contacts per year

D_i = distance in miles

b_0 and b_1 are unknown parameters.

This implies that

Equation 2, $\dfrac{dC_i}{dD_i} = b_0 b_1 D_i^{b_1 - 1}$

where $\dfrac{dC_i}{dD_i}$ is the derivative of C with respect to D, or the rate of change in C for a change in D. This model does have the property that the rate of change in contact frequency following a change in distance is presented as being proportional to distance, which can be seen from Equation 2.

In order to estimate the parameters of this equation by linear regression techniques it is necessary to make the additional assumption that the errors in the model are multiplicative, rather than additive, as they were in the linear model. (See Goldberger, 1964:215; Johnson, 1963:45). The parameters b_0 and b_1 can then be estimated by writing equation 1 as:

Equation 3, $C_i = b_0 D_i^{b_1} e_i$

and taking the logarithm of both sides of equation 3. (In all computations natural logs are used.) The parameters $\ln b_0$ and b_1 of the resulting equation,

Equation 4, $\ln C_i = \ln b_0 + b_1 \ln D_i + \ln e_i$,

can then be estimated by linear regression procedures.

A Further Assumption

Before discussing the data themselves it would be useful to discuss a further, perhaps controversial, assumption. The models discussed here both assume that the frequency of contact is caused by distance between residences, rather than the reverse. One could justifiably argue that the desire to maintain or increase contact with kin causes an individual to remain close or to move closer to them. This would suggest that the desire for contact (or some more general measure of family ties) was a cause of both residential propinquity and frequent kin contact. Both would be simultaneous dependent variables and would be functions of other variables such as measures of familial commitment, some of which would affect both dependent variables.

Even though some individuals may change their residence in response to changes in familial commitment, however, it is also likely that for many others distance from kin is fixed, at least in the short run, by earlier decisions (such as choice of job) which are not subject to rapid fluctuation. One might argue, however, that one such decision, which may chronologically precede the choice of job, is the decision to remain close to one's family. For those who give family ties priority over occupational demands, the choice of job location may be limited by the decision to remain near one's family. Another possibility is that familial commitment and distance from one's family affect each other over time in a process in which decreasing strength of family ties, caused by age and other commitments (e.g., to the family of procreation) allows one to move further away from parents. Increased distance, in turn, leads to less frequent interaction with parents, which entails further diminution of the emotional ties to them; and so on. This process and the others mentioned above are all possibilities which cannot be tested with the present data, which are cross-sectional. We can only assume that, over any short period of time, distance must operate as a fixed cost of kin contact, regardless of the strength of family ties. It is the effect of this cost factor which is in question in the present research. I have, therefore, assumed that in the case of a given individual the cost (in terms of distance) of visiting a given relative is fixed in the short run—that is, in the period encompassed by the sample.

The Sample

The data of the present research were obtained from a national random quota sample of 1,469 adults, secured in a survey conducted in 1965 by the National Opinion Research Center. (For a detailed discussion of this method of sampling, see Sudman, 1966.) Respondents were asked a series of questions about eight male relatives, including father, oldest brother (who might be younger than the respondent, or older than he), a male cousin, husband of oldest married sister, mother's oldest brother, father's oldest brother, mother's father, and father's father. The questions covered basic demographic information such as age, occupation, education. In addition, regarding each relative the respondent was asked "Where does he live?" and "How often do you see him?" The last two variables, which are of present concern, were coded as follows:

Residential Distance

Relatives Living in Same City as Respondent — 1 Mile
Relatives Living Outside City but Within United States, Canada, or
    Mexico — Number of Highway Miles [3]
Relatives Living in Foreign Countries — Number of Airline Miles [4]

Kin Contact Frequency (coded in times per year)

Every Day — 365
Two or Three Times a Week — 130
Once a Week — 52
Two or Three Times a Month — 30
Eight to Twelve Times a Year — 10
Four to Eight Times a Year — 6
Two or Three Times a Year — 2.5
Once a Year or Less — 1

Throughout this study the analysis is limited to married males. The information on contact with parents includes data on the respondents who were married men and on the husbands of married female respondents. Data on the latter were available because respondents reported their spouses' characteristics and contacts, as well as their own. There are 1,061 husbands in the total sample. However, the sample used in different parts of the analysis varies considerably in size, depending on the availability of the relative in question. The analysis of contacts with relatives other than parents is based on the reports of married male respondents only, because data were not available on the relatives of their spouses.

Some readers may question my decision to limit the analysis to married males, especially since women are usually regarded as more active in maintaining family ties. I had two reasons for doing so: First, the original survey on which the analysis is based asked questions about male relatives only. Since I assumed that the contacts of married women are predominantly with other women, it would be misleading to study their contacts with their male relatives for that would undoubtedly lead to underestimation of the amount of kin contact, and might introduce, as well, an unmeasurable bias in the nature of the contacts reported. Secondly, the present data are particularly appropriate in assessing the effects, demonstrated in the sociological literature, of occupational status and mobility on kinship ties, being based on a national sample and containing detailed information on occupation. Since the vast majority of women are not employed in remunerative occupations, and the significance of a husband's occupation to his wife's kinship contacts is ambiguous, I decided to limit the analysis to males. I have included only married males because the literature holds out virtually no expectations about the contacts of unmarried males (or females) — a subject worth a study in itself.

Limitations of the Data

Despite the fact that these data are more detailed than any hitherto published on kin contact, they suffer from several limitations which should be described, since they are relevant to the evaluation of the goodness of fit of the models proposed and since knowledge of present limitations may warn future analysts.

In the first place, the contact variable (which is the same in the case of each relative) does not distinguish between the party initiating the contact and the party receiving it. Although we assume that more frequent contact indicates greater commitment to relatives, the commitment of an individual who travels ten miles to see his parents every day is quite different from that of one whose parents travel ten miles every day to visit *him*. Although the latter situation still indicates strong family ties, the respondents' motivation, or lack of it, in the two cases is probably dissimilar. In addition, the present contact variable does not allow the determination of where the contact takes place nor does it tell anything about the nature of the contact. One who sees his relative every day may see him in a variety of circumstances, ranging, for example, from the workplace, to the home of either, to a local bar. The importance of these contacts in indicating familial commitment is undoubtedly relative.

A somewhat more serious limitation is that the codes do not distinguish between those who see a relative once a year, those who see him less than once a year, and those who never see him. Thus the measure of contact is artificially truncated (see discussion in Appendix F). Furthermore, those who say they never see their kin are likely to be a distinctive but small subpopulation, subject to influences unlike those affecting others.[5]

Another subset of the respondents who live in the same city as a given relative and report seeing him every day are not affected by an independent variable, since they live together; the most likely instance is the case of parents who live in the household of the respondent. The problem may be substantial in the present data. The data on contacts and distance to father of all husbands in the sample for whom these facts are known,[6] reveals that of 188 husbands who live in the same city as their fathers, 47, or 25 percent, see them every day. According to the 1960 U.S. Census, the percentage of husband-wife households in which the parents of the head or of the spouse of the head of household are present is .0436.[7] Approximately half of these (or .0218) might then be households in which the parents of the husband are present. An even smaller perecentage might be households where the husband's father is present. If .0218 is taken as a maximum and applied to the total sample of husbands (N = 1,061), which includes both those with living fathers and those whose fathers are not alive, this then would mean that an estimated maximum of 23 of the total of 1,061 husbands have their fathers living with them. Thus 23 of the 47 husbands whose fathers are alive, who live in the same city as their fathers, and who report seeing them every day, could be husbands whose fathers live with them.

One further shortcoming is that my use of contacts per year is arbitrary, since a person may report no contacts within a given year but could have seen his relatives just a little longer ago. This problem could be eliminated by using a more exact measure and by expanding the period of time covered by the measure; however, that might introduce a new problem, for if the period is extended too far it may encompass and mask real changes in frequency of contact characteristic of phases of the life cycle.

The distance variable too, is inadequate since it does not distinguish between distances within the city.[8] Consequently, intra-city variations in contact cannot be attributed to distance, even though some of them may well be due to it. Again, if other independent variables are independent of distance, this will not affect the estimates of their effects. It will merely leave unexplained that variance which is due to distance.

Findings

In the present chapter, only contacts with husband's father will be analyzed. It is hoped that a detailed analysis of that relationship will establish the general form it takes in the case of other relatives as well, so that parameters can then be estimated without having to start from the very beginning with each one. In order to give the reader some idea of the frequency of contact between husbands and their fathers, the appropriate percentage distribution is presented in Table 1.1.

TABLE 1.1

Percentage Distribution of Contacts per Year
Between Husbands and Their Fathers

Contacts per Year								
365	130	52	30	10	6	2.5	1	Total
13.20%	16.14%	16.87%	9.78%	9.29%	5.13%	8.80%	20.78%	99.99% N = 409

Of husbands whose fathers reside in the same city, the percentage who visit at least once a week is 77.66%. Adams (1968:39) found that among males in Greensboro, North Carolina, whose parents live in Greensboro, the comparable figure was 81 percent. In Aiken's data, collected in Detroit (1964:69), the percentage of respondent households in which at least one member sees the husband's parents living in Detroit but not in the same household at least once or twice a week, the figure is 58 percent. Other studies report the frequency of contact with relatives, but most of them do not provide sufficient detail (in terms of relatives visited or of frequency of visiting) to yield comparable figures. Even the figures cited here are not strictly comparable. However, they do indicate some similarity across samples.

A rough idea of the distribution in terms of distance can be obtained from Table 1.2. It should be noted that the category intervals differ considerably in size.

TABLE 1.2

Percentage Distribution of Residential Distance
Between Husbands and Their Fathers

Range of Distance in Miles							
Same City	2-19	20-49	50-149	150-299	300-999	1000-6800	Total
45.96%	9.29%	8.56%	7.33%	6.60%	9.78%	12.47%	99.99% N = 409

The distribution is obviously skewed, with the percentage of persons in a given category of distance decreasing as distance increases.

The regression estimates of the parameters in the proportional model shown in Equation 4 are as follows:

Equation 5. $\qquad \ln C_i = 4.482 - .566 \ln D_i$

Adequacy of the Model

Both the substantive considerations mentioned earlier of the effect of distance on frequency of contact and an empirical comparison of a linear with a proportional model lead to the conclusion that a proportional model which predicts the natural logarithm of contacts from the natural logarithm of distance is much better than a linear model which predicts actual frequency of contact from actual distance (See the complete comparison of these models in Appendix F). Briefly, the proportional model explains considerably more variance than does the linear model; the predicted values of contact at different points in the range of distance are much closer to the observed mean frequencies of contact in those ranges in the proportional model than in the linear model; and the linear model has the additional disadvantage of predicting negative frequencies of contact at great distances. These negative values are meaningless, since contacts per year cannot be less than zero; in the logarithmic or proportional model they cannot occur.

Although the proportional model is more adequate than the linear, it is by no means established as the correct one. Nor have any statements been made about the relationship between the parameters estimated with this model and the true parameters of the population from which the sample was drawn. In order to make such statements assumptions must be made about the distribution of errors in this model. If it can be assumed that each of the log errors comes from a population which is normally distributed with a mean 0 and variance σ^2 (a constant), then hypotheses can be tested and confidence intervals established for the estimated parameters.

Although it is not necessary for present purposes that the assumptions of lognormality and constant error variance be met, evidence of the validity of these assumptions would be extremely useful in establishing the parental contact—distance relationship as one of a general class of relationships in which the disturbances are lognormally distributed. In these relationships the amount of response to a stimulus is proportional to the magnitude of the stimulus. If changes in distance are regarded as stimuli and changes in frequency of contact as responses, similarities can be established to a wide variety of phenomena, all of which fit this general model and many of which have been much more thoroughly studied than the one under consideration.[9] Furthermore, a considerable amount is known about the statistical properties of such distributions and the procedures for estmating their parameters. For example, many economic relationships are of the stimulus-response variety (e.g., changes in demand for a product as its price changes), and concepts employed in economic analysis may also prove useful in studying contact, as I point out later. Psychological data also often take the stimulus-response form, and techniques employed in psychology may be of use.

Given the limitations of the data under consideration, it would be unwise to place too much emphasis on testing either the assumption of normality or that of homoscedasticity of the error variance. However, a clue may at least be obtained as to the normality of the distribution of the log errors by examining the frequency distribution of the residuals (Table 1.3).

This histogram does give the impression of normality—an impression which persists in the middle distance categories when the residuals are distributed within distance categories. However, it should be pointed out that the residuals in the two tails of the distribution come from different parts of the distance range. In the left tail of the distribution there are no residuals generated at extremely great distances; and in the right tail there are none from the 0 in mile (same city) category. A more precise model might regard the distribution as log-normal throughout most of its range but limited at both ends by the impossibility of certain values of the dependent variable. However, for reasons discussed below, upper and lower bounds of the dependent variable can more easily be regarded as errors of coding and measurement rather than as conditions inherent to the nature of contact with kin.

Heteroscedasticity

The assumption that the errors each come from populations with constant variance σ^2 is important in determining the adequacy of the model. If the mean squared residuals in different parts of the distance range are not constant, then it may be appropriate to transform the variables to yield a relationship in which the errors are homoscedastic. Such transformations should provide more efficient estimates of the parameters—that is, estimates with

TABLE 1.3

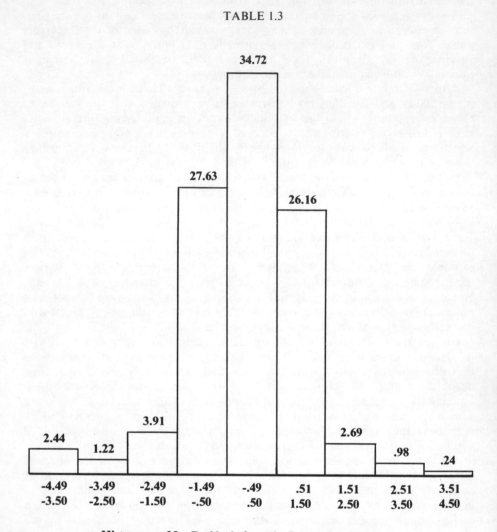

Histogram of Ln Residuals from the Proportional Model

smaller variances (Goldberger, 1964:235-236; Johnston, 1963:207-211). Making such transformations, however, requires knowledge of the form of the heteroscedasticity involved as well as the assumption that the variable as presently coded can be properly transformed. In this case it seems likely that the heteroscedasticity is due to a coding decision, in which case a transformation would be inappropriate.

TABLE 1.4

Mean Squared Ln Residuals in Ln Distance Ranges
for Proportional Model

Ln Distance Range	Mean Squared Ln Residuals	N
0.0 (Same City)	2.005	188
0.50 - 1.49	2.649	8
1.50 - 2.49	2.335	22
2.50 - 3.49	1.656	31
3.50 - 4.49	1.210	34
4.50 - 5.49	.822	28
5.50 - 6.49	.923	33
6.50 - 7.49	.609	42
7.50 - 8.82	.294	23

As Table 1.4 shows, the mean squared log residuals in different ranges of distance are not constant. In fact, Bartlett's test of the homogeneity of sample variances (Walker and Lev, 1953:193) applied to the variances of the errors in each category of distance around their category mean yields a X^2 value of 57.45. With eight degrees of freedom, this value indicates that the probability is less than .001 that these sample variances come from populations with the same variance. This finding is of substantive interest, particularly if applied to Adams' hypothesis that the variance in kin contact differs at different points in the distance range (Adams, 1968:39-40). Adams argues that the variance would be least at both ends of the range: at one end because of the obligation to visit one's kin, given the opportunity to do so; and at the other end because of the impediments imposed by distance. However, the means of the squared residuals shown here show no curvilinear tendency with distance, as Adams' hypothesis would lead us to expect.[10] They do show a tendency to decrease with increasing log distance, so that the greater distances have the smallest squared residuals.

If the mean squared errors were truly a function of distance, then the variables could be transformed to obtain a relationship with constant error variance.[11] However, the categories of greater distance are also those in which the expected values of contact are lowest. If it is recalled that the contact variable is collapsed at the lower end, so that all values less than or equal to 0 log contacts per year are combined, then a reason for these small mean squared residuals becomes apparent. The mean squared residuals of the greater distances are each based on observations of which a large proportion have the value 0, which is equivalent to one or fewer contacts per year. This proportion increases as distance increases. If the original contact variable were allowed to take on the values between 1 and 0 (as would occur if, for example, the number of contacts per year were averaged over a number of years) then the equivalent range of the log of contacts would be from

0 to $-\infty$. This would mean that the means of the squared log residuals would be considerably increased by the inclusion of large negative deviations. If this analysis is correct, then it would be inappropriate to transform the variables, for the inadequacy would lie with the coding rather than with the model itself.

Summary and Discussion

It is difficult to judge the adequacy of a model when its possible defects are confounded with defects in the coding and measurement of variables — as the tentative tone of the preceding discussion reflects. I have tried to demonstrate, on both intuitive and empirical grounds, that the relationship between distance and parental contact follows the general form of a stimulus-response pattern, in which the rate of change in contact accompanying a change in residential distance is proportional to the distance involved. A model incorporating this assumption explains almost 61 percent of the variance in log parental contact and predicts log contact frequency very close to the observed means in the various categories of distance. Furthermore, the means of the log deviations are close to zero in each distance category, and the overall distribution of the log deviations appears to approximate normality. Although the assumption of homoscedasticity of the error variance is not justified by the data, the departures from constant variance occur in the greatest distance categories, where the expected values of contact are smallest. These values are artificially bounded by zero due to coding, so that negative values are impossible. The mean squared residuals in these categories are thus artifically constrained.

Assuming that the frequency of kin contact is inherently limited, due to a phenomenon similar to saturation at the upper end, or to complete absence of contact at the lower end, and that there were large concentrations at either or both ends for these reasons, then models incorporating these assumptions could be constructed, if the lognormality of the error distribution could also be assumed in the rest of the range. [12] In the present case, however, it seems more reasonable to assume that individuals can see their relatives more than once a day and less than once a year. More precise measures in the future will, let us hope, allow for these possibilities. Meanwhile, the utility of the model established here will be demonstrated by its application in the following chapter, to the distance and contact relationships of respondents and their genealogically more distant relatives.

FOOTNOTES

[1] This is somewhat of a simplification of Parsons' argument. He does not imply a simple one-way determination of the kinship structure by the occupational system. In fact, he argues explicitly (1954:192) that there has been "a process of mutual accommodation between these two fundamental aspects of our social structure."

[2] Adams (1968:152) suggests that this is the case. The confounding of the effects of distance with other explanatory variables is actually a more general problem. For example, in discussing the segregated shopping patterns of a supposedly integrated area, Molotch remarks that "distance outweighs other possible considerations...in determining shopping patterns." (December, 1969:882). If residential distance explains the frequency of interracial as well as other contact, there is no need to look for further explanations.

[3] If relative lived within the state or in an adjacent state, respondent was asked the exact number of miles. For nonadjacent states and cases where respondent did not know mileage, the distance was computed by coders in miles, from the Rand McNally *Standard Highway Mileage Guide.*

[4] Distances were estimated from the table of "Airline Distances between Principal Cities of the World" in the New York World-Telegram's *World Almanac and Book of Facts* (1963: 766).

[5] In fact, at least one analyst (Aiken, 1964: 39-40) eliminates from his analysis households in the Detroit area which were never visited by members of respondent households.

[6] This sample includes data for the respondent if the respondent was a married or widowed male and data for the respondent's spouse if the respondent was a married female.

[7] *United States Census of Population, 1960,* PC(2)-4A, Table 17, p. 168.

[8] All distances from relatives living in the same city as respondent were coded as one mile. In the original data with which I worked they had all been arbitrarily coded as zero miles. I changed them to the equally arbitrary distance of one mile to make it possible to convert them to logarithms. (The natural log of one is zero, whereas the natural log of zero is minus infinity.)

[9] See Aitchison and Brown's discussion of such phenomena and methods of studying them (1957, especially Chapter 7).

[10] One major reason why Adams' hypothesis should fail to be supported by the present research is that Adams was dealing with a rather homogeneous population (white residents of Greensboro, married, married only once, and for 20 years or less). One would not expect to find in this sample the extremes of variation in distance or kin contact that one finds in a national random sample.

[11] This would be analogous to Goldberger's transformation of the savings-income relationship, where the disturbance variance is assumed to be proportional to the square of income (1964: 235-236). In the present case, however, the resulting transformed equation would have two terms involving distance with coefficients to be estimated, and the problem of heteroscedasticity might simply be exchanged for one of collinearity. If we were looking at the errors from a linear model when the true model was proportional, we might expect the error variances to decrease with increasing distance. This tendency, however, should be eliminated in the log errors.

[12] For one such model, see Tobin (1958) and Rosett (1959).

CHAPTER 2

DISTANCE AND
KIN CONTACT

Introduction

Although there has been no systematic quantitative study of the effect of distance on kin contacts, many observations have been made and many hypotheses suggested about the relative strength of ties to various categories of relatives and the possible effect of distance on contacts with kinfolk of varying degrees of relationship. In regard to the relative strength of ties to relatives, for example, Cumming and Schneider (1961:500) conclude from intensive interviews with fifteen adults that first cousins are as intimate, judged in terms of knowing each other's names, as are uncles and aunts. Garigue, studying French Canadians (1956:1090), reports that frequency of contact is greatest between members of the same generation. Shaw (1954), whose observations are based on interviews with 101 families in a London suburb, emphasizes the importance of the maternal grandmother in the lives of many of the families. Sussman (1959:33) is convinced that intergenerational kin ties are particularly important in the lives of urban families. Adams (1968: 134) finds, in his sample of married adults in Greensboro, that 28 percent of his sample spend more time with aunts and uncles than with cousins or grandparents. However, he points out that the majority have no living grandparents, which tells us nothing about those who do. Robins and Tomanec (1962), using a combined measure of "closeness of interaction," find that grandparents are closer to Ego than are aunts and uncles, cousins, and great aunts and uncles. These observations illustrate the idea that there are, or are assumed to be, systematic differences in the strength of kinship ties, based on categories of relatives. However, they do not offer much empirical evidence about the ordering of kinship categories in terms of frequency of contact or other measures.

There are a few studies which do try to compare the frequency of contact with various relatives. My computations from Aiken's data (1964:59) on frequency of contact with husbands' relatives who do live inside the Detroit area (where the respondents live) indicate that, of the relatives comparable to those in the present study, parents are seen most frequently, followed by siblings, grandparents, uncles and aunts, and cousins, in that order. Of relatives outside the Detroit area the order is the same (1964:63), except that cousins are seen slightly more frequently than aunts and uncles.[1] Firth, Hubert and Forge (1969:200) remark (but do not demonstrate) that in their study of two areas in North London, contact is maintained with a slightly higher percentage of kins of the parental generation than of first cousins. Again, the availability of these kin is not controlled. Reiss's data, collected in Boston (1962:335), show that interaction is most frequent in the parent-child relationship; siblings are second; grandparent-child, uncle, aunt-niece, nephew relationships (combined) are third; and cousins are fourth.

Distance and Contact

The hypotheses about the relationship between distance and differential contact with various relatives are based primarily on two considerations. Those who suggest that distance is more important to less closely related relatives usually do so on the ground that closely related kin will maintain contact in spite of distance, the effect of which will be more prohibitive to the more distantly related (Garigue, 1956:1094, for example). A similar argument is sometimes advanced regarding the effect of status and/or religious difference on contact with more distant relatives, in whose case such differences are assumed to be more discouraging of contact (for example, Bott, 1957:144). The hypothesis that distance is less important in determining contact with more distantly related kin usually arises from the observation that such contact is either incidental or contingent on visits to closer relatives who happen to live in the same place. For example, Adams (1968:145) remarks that "Cousin contact is frequently, we find, a result of the combination opportunity (sic) of incidental interaction appended to a visit with the kin of orientation." Contacts with more distant kin are presumed to occur on ritualistic or ceremonial occasions such as weddings, funerals, Christmas, and reunions, as many students have observed.[2] In either case, contingent or ritual contact, frequency would not be determined by distance, especially if there is no obligation to see genealogically distant relatives frequently even if they are close at hand. According to some analysts, the element of choice or selectivity in kin contact operates to a much greater extent in the case of siblings and more distant relatives than in that of parents, so that even relatives living quite close by need not be seen more than minimally.[3] All these considerations, however, suggest that the variance explained by distance should be smaller in the case of more distant relatives; they do not necessarily imply that the slope of the relationship should be less.

Elasticity of Contact

A somewhat different way to formulate hypotheses about the magnitude of the effect of distance on contact with diverse relatives is suggested by the concept, "elasticity." Elasticity is defined as the ratio of a percentage change in one variable to a percentage change in another variable. It is used most commonly by economists, who are interested in, for example, the percentage change in demand for a commodity with a given percentage change in its cost. If the demand for a commodity quadruples when its price is cut in half, that commodity has twice as much elasticity as one the demand for which doubles when its price is cut in half.

The concept of elasticity can also be applied to the relationship between distance and kin contact. If distance reflects the cost of contact, then the demand for visits to given relatives should decrease as distance from them increases. However, the percentage change in frequency of contact following a percentage change in distance could differ with different relatives.

It is important at this point to note a feature of the double-log model developed in the preceding chapter which makes it particularly appropriate both for economic analysis and for the present problem. In a linear model and in most other models, the amount of elasticity of a commodity differs at different points on the cost range. That is, the percentage change in demand for a percentage change in price depends on the prive involved. However, in the double-log model elasticity is constant at all levels of the price range. Furthermore, elasticity can be shown to be measured by the coefficient of

$$\ln C_i = b_0 + b_1 \ln D_i.^4$$

The fact that elasticity is a constant in this model means that we can compare the relative elasticities of contacts with diverse relatives without regard to the various distances involved.

Hypotheses about Elasticity

The concept of elasticity is suggestive of at least two contradictory hypotheses. One hypothesis is based on an assumption stated by Samuelson (1958: 372): that the demand for a product drops as its price rises because people will begin to substitute other products if such products are available; e.g., tea for coffee. Thus, the greater the "substitutability" of a product, the greater should be its elasticity. "Substitutability" is very similar to the concept of "functional equivalence," used in sociological jargon. The more functional equivalents there are of face-to-face contact, the greater the elasticity of contact, since a functional equivalent can be substituted for a visit whenever distance becomes too great. On the assumption that the maintenance of familial relationships is necessary and that other forms of contact can be substituted for the face-to-face type (as Litwak, 1960, for example, claims; see also Litwak and Szelenyi, 1969), we would expect to find that the contacts of those relatives for whom the greatest number of substitute mechanisms (such as telephone calls, gifts, letters and the like) are available would show the greatest elasticity. In this case, parents should show the greatest elasticity; and in general, the closer the relationship the greater the elasticity of visiting. Closer relationships, such as that of parent and child, are more diffuse or multifaceted, and therefore have more bases of interaction to begin with. Because of the importance of their relationship, parents and children are more likely to develop and make use of mechanisms of indirect contact in order to maintain flexibility in the face of necessary separation than are more distantly related individuals who have less reason to maintain their relationship and fewer mechanisms for doing so, and whose contacts, therefore, show less elasticity or response to changes in distance. It is noteworthy that, in a different context, Firth, Hubert and Forge (1969:122) speak of kinship as "elastic, not needing nearby residence nor continual operational expression to maintain it."

Another way to develop the same hypothesis, without relying on the substitutability of mechanisms of direct and indirect contact, is to consider the likelihood of an ongoing normative system or system of mutual expectations between respondents and various categories of relatives. The mere existence of such a system increases the possibility of weighing the claims of obligations against the counter-claims of cost (distance). This basis of more or less rational decision-making is more likely in relationships with intimate kin (i.e., members of the family of orientation), among whom, therefore, changes in frequency of contact should be more responsive to changes in distance. (Rational is used here in the sense of altering one's behavior to adapt to changing conditions, so that the means used are appropriate to the ends desired.)

The alternative hypothesis assumes, in common with the preceding hypothesis, that it is more essential to maintain the closer relationships. However, it postulates that for this purpose face-to-face contact is necessary or obligatory. One can assume, in developing this hypothesis, either that there are no functional equivalents of face-to-face contact or that rational considerations of cost are less likely to be taken into account when decisions regarding contact involve more intimate kin. On the basis of either assumption we would expect contacts with parents to show the least elasticity. Since the parent-child relationship is, presumably, the most necessary, visits to parents would be maintained at a relatively high level of frequency regardless of changes in distance, whereas contacts with other relatives would be more subject to the costs of distance and would show a greater proportional change in response to a proportional change in distance.

Findings

The percentage distributions of residential distance and contact of the eight relatives available for study will now be presented for men in the sample who have the relative in question. Naturally, the samples are somewhat different for each relative, since not all male respondents had living relatives of every designation. The samples also differ from the one used in the previous chapter, where the data were on married respondents if the respondent was male and on respondent's spouse if respondent was female. Unfortunately, data on the relatives of spouses were not available for most of the categories of relatives, so in the present chapter I have used data on male respondents only.

The percentage distributions of distance from each relative are presented in Table 2.1. The relatives are ordered by increasing mean ln distance from respondent. These means are F (2.525), FF (3.053), OB (3.303), HOMS (3.496), MC (3.632), MF (3.666), FOB (4.074), MOB (4.470). (See notation key in Table 2.1.)

The table does show differences in distance between residences of various relatives—which, however, probably stem from many different sources. Since

TABLE 2.1

Percentage Distributions of Distances Between Residences of Male
Respondents and Eight Male Relatives

Relative*	Distance in Miles							Total	N
	Same City	2-19	20-49	50-149	150-299	300-999	1000-8999		
F	49.79	7.59	6.75	6.33	8.02	12.66	8.86	100.00	237
FF	36.84	10.53	10.53	5.26	5.26	26.32	5.26	100.00	19
OB	40.34	6.34	6.05	5.76	8.93	16.14	16.43	99.99	347
HOMS	35.35	9.24	5.10	7.01	11.46	15.29	16.56	100.01	314
MC	31.46	8.82	6.41	10.82	11.02	15.83	15.63	99.99	499
MF	22.50	17.50	7.50	17.50	7.50	15.00	12.50	100.00	40
FOB	26.53	9.52	7.48	7.48	8.16	19.05	21.77	99.99	147
MOB	19.56	7.11	8.00	10.67	14.22	20.44	20.00	100.00	225

*Notation: F — Father; FF — Father's Father; OB — Oldest Brother; HOMS — Husband of Oldest Married Sister; MC — Male Cousin; MF — Mother's Father; FOB — Father's Oldest Brother; MOB — Mother's Oldest Brother.

respondent's immediate family has ordinarily grown up with him, the percentage who are still located in the same city should be higher than the percentage of nonmembers of the family of orientation. There seems to be a tendency for respondent to live closer to the paternal side of his family than the maternal, judging from the disparities in data as between fathers' and mothers' fathers, and fathers' and mothers' oldest brothers.[5] The mean of male cousin is probably higher than if it were an average of all cousins, since respondent was allowed to give data for any male cousin (preferably the one closest in age), and he probably chose one living close by, rather than one more remote. (The same bias may exist in Aiken's data, 1964:59, which show that the percentage of husband's cousins named by the respondents who live in the Detroit area is as high as the percentage of husband's parents who do so.) Aiken's data on husband's relatives show 54 percent of parents, 54 percent of cousins, 48 percent of brothers, 44 percent of sisters, 39 percent of uncles, and 31 percent of grandparents living in the Detroit area. These percentages are somewhat higher than mine of comparable categories of relatives in the "same city" category. However, if the categories, "same city" and "2-9 miles" (the latter not presented in Table 2.1) are combined in order to increase comparability, we find the enlarged category contains 53.2 percent of husbands' fathers, 36.1 percent of chosen male cousins, 44.7 percent of oldest brothers, 41.1 percent of husbands of oldest married sisters, 30.6 percent of fathers' fathers, and 30.0 percent of mothers' fathers.

Some of these figures, particularly those on close relatives, are quite similar to Aiken's.

TABLE 2.2

Percentage Distributions of Contacts per Year Between Male
Respondents and Eight Male Relatives

Relative*	Contacts per Year								Total	N
	365	130	52	30	10	6	2.5	1		
F	25.32	15.61	11.81	6.75	8.02	5.06	5.49	21.94	100.00	237
FF	---	26.32	5.26	15.79	--	10.53	10.53	31.58	100.01	19
OB	8.93	11.53	10.66	6.63	8.65	6.34	10.66	36.60	100.00	347
HOMS	6.05	6.37	7.01	9.55	11.78	8.28	13.06	37.90	100.00	314
MF	--	--	7.50	22.50	15.00	12.50	10.00	32.50	100.00	40
MC	2.81	4.81	5.21	5.61	12.22	6.21	12.83	50.30	100.00	499
FOB	3.40	2.72	6.12	6.12	10.20	8.84	8.16	54.42	99.98	147
MOB	.89	2.67	5.33	4.00	8.44	7.11	11.56	60.00	100.00	225

*See Table 2.1 for notation.

The percentage distributions of contacts with relatives are presented in Table 2.2. Relatives are ordered by decreasing mean log contacts: F (3.275), FF (2.311), OB (2.145), HOMS (1.808), MF (1.722), MC (1.306), FOB (1.251), MOB (.956). Not surprisingly, the decreasing mean log contacts are ordered in the same way as the increasing mean log distances, except for a reversal of mother's father and male cousin. Without taking into account the differences in distance underlying these differences in frequency of contact we can say little about the differences in contact as it concerns various relatives. Nor can we establish whether the effect of distance on kin contact differs as between kin categories.

Refining the Model

As mentioned previously, the distance variable does not distinguish distance in the case of those who live in the same city as their parents or other relatives. This becomes a problem when we compare the elasticity of contacts. Since a large percentage of the sample of each relative is found in the "same city" category where there is no variation in distance, the mean frequency of contact of this category could dominate the regression. The slope of the regression line (which is the elasticity) will be heavily influenced by a single point where from 20 to 50 percent of the sample is concentrated (see Table 2.1); and the difference in elasticity will be determined partly by differences in mean contacts in the "same city" category. We can avoid this problem by computing the regressions using only individuals who are not in the same city as the relative in question, since we cannot compute a slope for those in the "same city" category, where distances are treated as all alike.[6] If we do this on the sample of husbands' contacts with fathers studied in Chapter I, we find that the new regression equation is:

$$\ln C_i = 5.278 - .704 \ln D_i$$

The original regression equation was:

$$\ln C_i = 4.482 - .566 \ln D_i$$

Both the slope and the intercept have increased, and the percentage of variance explained has gone up slightly from 62.6 percent to 65.0 percent. The fact that there are differences in the slopes and intercepts indicates the importance of separating those in the "same city" category from those in other categories in the analysis of the effects of other variables, at least initially, since the latter may also have different effects in the two categories, especially if correlated with distance.

Elasticities of Relatives

We can now examine the estimates of the relationship between distance and contact with kin. They are regression estimates from the refined version of the double-log model developed in Chapter I, based only on respondents who live in a different city from the relative in question. As was pointed out above, the double-log model has the feature of constant elasticity, which led to the hypotheses regarding the elasticity of contacts with various relatives (that is, the percentage change in contact accompanying a percentage change in distance). It was suggested that contacts with more closely related kin would show greater elasticity than contacts with kin more distantly related, either because of the greater likelihood of norms which allow rational decision-making or because of the greater likelihood of there being mechanisms of indirect contact to compensate for the necessary separation of members of the family. Either situation would allow them to respond more readily to reduced face-to-face contact when the cost of it (in terms of distance) becomes too great. Alternatively, if face-to-face contact is considered necessary to the maintenance of familial relationships, regardless of distance, then we would expect distance to have less effect on contact with more closely related kin.

Data to test these hypotheses are presented in Table 2.3 in which relatives are ordered by decreasing slopes or elasticities. An elasticity coefficient of -.6 can be interpreted to mean that a 10 percent increase in distance brings about a 6 percent decrease in contact. The elasticities in Table 2.3 do show a strong tendency to decrease with increasing genealogical distance from respondent. Father has the highest elasticity, followed by oldest brother and brother-in-law (HOMS), then by maternal and paternal grandparents and male cousin, while maternal and paternal uncle fall together at the bottom. Thus the order of decreasing elasticity goes from parents to siblings (and husbands of siblings), then to grandparents, cousins, and uncles. The differences in samples and the small size of some of the N's call for caution in the interpreting of differences between individual relatives; however, the general conclusion

TABLE 2.3

Intercepts and Slopes (Elasticities) for the Relationship of Ln Contacts
to Ln Distance, Estimated for Individuals for Whom $Ln\ D_i \neq 0$.
Estimates for Eight Male Relatives of Male Respondents

Relative*	Intercept	Slope (Elasticity)	N
F	5.726	-.787	119
OB	4.384	-.610	207
HOMS	4.064	-.560	203
MF	3.617	-.466	31
FF	3.396	-.429	12
MC	2.723	-.381	342
MOB	2.424	-.331	181
FOB	2.400	-.314	108

*See Table 2.1 for notation.

that more closely-related kin show greater elasticity in face-to-face contact
is definitely substantiated.

Comparisons of the slopes and intercepts of different relatives may be
facilitated by Figure 2.1, which presents the regression lines in graphic form,
along with approximate mile and contact equivalents of ln miles and ln
contacts. Because of the differences in slopes, differences in frequency of
contact among relatives become smaller as distance increases. This means
that at very great distances one can visit a relative very seldom, regardless
of how close the relative is genealogically. The diagram also shows that individuals throughout most of the distance range still contact father more frequently than any other relative, since the regression line for father does not
intersect any other line until $ln\ D \doteq 6.55$ ($\doteq 699$ miles). Since fewer than 22
percent of the sample live more than 300 miles from their fathers (see Table
2.1), this greater frequency of visits to father holds true of more than 78
percent.

The Element of Choice

One other hypothesis was mentioned earlier and can be tested with the
present data, namely, that the element of choice or the lack of obligation is
greater among genealogically more distant relatives (see footnote 3). Operationally, this hypothesis could have various interpretations. One possible
interpretation is that visits to less closely related kin are more random—i.e.,
less determinate—than visits to more intimate kin. If this is so, then distance
(and perhaps other factors as well) should explain less variance for more distantly related kin. This hypothesis can be tested in the case of persons outside the "same city" category, by comparing the R^2's of the regressions of
ln contact on ln distance. If the hypothesis is supported, the proportion of
variation explained by distance would be expected to decrease with increasing

FIGURE 2.1

Regression Lines for Ln Contact on Ln Distance for Eight Male Relatives of Male Respondents
(Intercepts and Slopes are Given in Table 2.5)

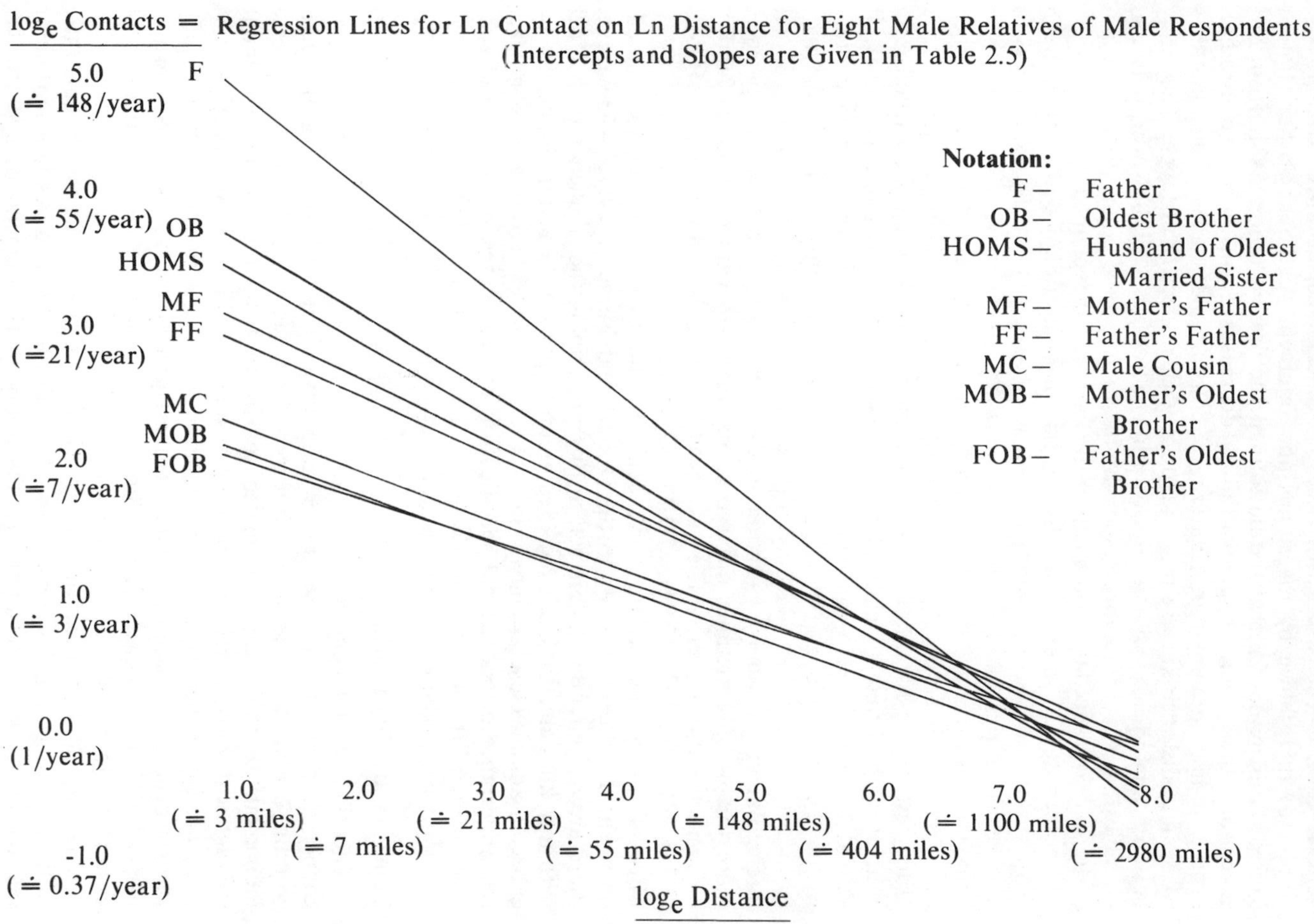

$\log_e$ Contacts =
5.0 (≐ 148/year)
4.0 (≐ 55/year)
3.0 (≐21/year)
2.0 (≐7/year)
1.0 (≐ 3/year)
0.0 (1/year)
-1.0 (≐ 0.37/year)
F
OB
HOMS
MF
FF
MC
MOB
FOB
1.0 (≐ 3 miles)
2.0 (≐ 7 miles)
3.0 (≐ 21 miles)
4.0 (≐ 55 miles)
5.0 (≐ 148 miles)
6.0 (≐ 404 miles)
7.0 (≐ 1100 miles)
8.0 (≐ 2980 miles)
$\log_e$ Distance
Notation:
F— Father
OB— Oldest Brother
HOMS— Husband of Oldest Married Sister
MF— Mother's Father
FF— Father's Father
MC— Male Cousin
MOB— Mother's Oldest Brother
FOB— Father's Oldest Brother

genealogical distance. These R^2's are as follows: F (.624), OB (.568), HOMS (.549), MF (.368), MC (.298), MOB (.283), FOB (.270), and FF (.226). In general, they do decrease with increasing genealogical distance. The order is similar to that shown by the slopes and intercepts, although father's father (based on an N of 12) is at the bottom of the present order. Aside from this exception, the order of predictability decreases from father to brother, brother-in-law, grandparent (maternal), cousin, and uncles. Thus contacts with more distance kin are more random with respect to distance. They may be more random also with respect to other factors, as well; however, it is also possible that they are more responsive to factors other than distance, especially since distance leaves so much of the variance unexplained.

Another way to interpret the hypothesis of greater choice in contacts with more distant kin is to assume that it means that, given equally easy access to diverse categories of relatives, individuals are likely to vary more in their behavior toward more distantly related kin because here they are governed by norms which are weaker and less likely to produce uniform behavior. A crude test of the hypothesis can be obtained by comparing the variances in contact with different relatives in the "same city" category. However, it should be kept in mind that some of the differences in variation in contact within the city could also be explained by differences in variation in distance from various relatives, and any differences we find in variation in contact might still be caused by variation in distance within the city. In any case, there are no interpretable differences between kin categories in variability in contact within the city. The variances are as follows: FOB (3.44), HOMS (3.25), MC (3.03), OB (2.96), MOB (2.92), F (2.10), FF (1.43), and MF (.77). The lack of meaningful difference could be due to the situation just stated, or it could indicate that, as Firth, Hubert and Forge (1969:451-453) argue, there are no generally understood norms prescribing the frequency of contact with any kin categories, so that greater uniformity of behavior should not be expected among closely related kin. These alternative interpretations indicate the importance of operational specification of hypotheses and of careful consideration of the relationship between the operational definitions and the substantive hypotheses being tested.

Summary and Discussion

The findings on contact with various categories of kin reported in this chaper have necessarily been more suggestive than conclusive, for the data contain coding and measurement errors and the samples involve diverse individuals so that caution is called for in applying the conclusions about contact with various relatives to a particular individual. Contacts with relatives are interdependent, and individuals' contacts with their relatives may form a behavioral system, as Firth, Hubert and Forge (1969:450), for example, state. For this reason, the findings of this chapter should be thought of as applying to the population as a whole.

One may think of the demand for relatives in the population in much the same way as economists think of the demand for commodities in a particular market. In neither case do the results apply to the demand of a particular individual for each commodity or relative involved. The economic analogy also suggests the use of the concept of elasticity to describe the rate of change in contact accompanying change in distance. I hypothesized that the elasticity of contacts with more closely related kin would be greater than that with kin more distantly related, and the findings obtained do definitely rule out the possibility that visits to closer kin show *less* elasticity with regard to distance. They are not visited frequently regardless of distance. Thus the evidence suggests that contacts with closer kin are decided upon rationally, behavior being readily adapted to change in an external condition, namely, changes in cost.

This concept of elasticity and the general framework of rationality may well be useful in describing and testing other hypotheses about family patterns of choice and kinship behavior. If the proposition is accepted that greater elasticity in frequency of contact with relation to distance indicates a greater element of rationality in decisions, then comparisons between the elasticities of kin categories in diverse kinship systems, subcultures, and the like, can lead to inferences about the relative extent of rational choice in their kinship behavior.

This form of analysis can also be applied to other than face-to-face contact. In the present case, distance is an obvious and easily measured indicator of cost. If meaningful measures of the cost of other forms of contact were developed, then the relationship between demand for family contact in relation to its cost — in terms of time, money, commitment, etc. — could be analyzed.

Other problems involving fact-to-face contact may be analyzed in this way, and some of them will be examined in a later chapter. For example, Firth, Hubert and Forge (1969:13), Cumming and Schneider (1961), Garigue (1956), Townsend (1955:190), and Willmott and Young (1960:53-57) all argue that relatives are to some extent functionally equivalent to one another, either because contact with any of them allows one to fulfill his obligations, or because the needs which they satisfy are not tied to a particular category of kin. If this is true, the demand for a given relative as measured by visits to him might be expected to reduce the demand for another relative as the costs of visiting each of them change. This also depends, of course, on the distance between the two relatives and whether it is possible to see them simultaneously. This hypothesis is contradicted by the theory that relatives provide connecting links to other relatives,[7] so that contacting one relative increases the probability of contacting another. (The distinction drawn here is similar to that which economists draw between "complementary" and "competitive" products; however, the substantive reasons for complementarity or competitiveness of relatives should be kept in mind.)

A better argument could perhaps be made for trade-offs between relatives and nonrelatives. As distance from kin increases, nonrelatives may begin to replace relatives in functions which require propinquity. This form of analysis could also lead to inferences as to the specific functions which relatives and friends fulfill by determining which relatives and/or friends are linked in an exchange or trade-off system.[8] Since such relationships or functional equivalents may be normatively determined, especially in nonliterate societies, we might again expect to find differences in the relationship between demand for various relatives and for relatives as opposed to nonrelatives among subgroups of the population, for example, between males and females.

FOOTNOTES

[1]Aiken does not give any measure of central tendency. In order to make comparisons I scored the categories by rank order and computed means from the percentages.

[2]See the descriptions by Firth, Hubert and Forge (1969, Ch. 8) and Loudon (1961), for example. For an anthropological description of family reunions, see Ayoub (1966) and for a description of the meetings of groups of Jewish descent in New York City, see Mitchell (1961).

[3]Adams speaks of the greater element of choice in sibling, as compared with parental relations (1968:122). Firth, Hubert and Forge regard the "element of personal idiosyncrasy" as being "most marked in regard to affines . . . and particularly with the consanguines of affines," (1969: 173). Garigue reports a larger element of choice between members of the same generation than between generations (1956:1090). The behavior over which choice is exercised, however, differs from study to study.

[4]Elasticity is the ratio of a change in Y to a change in X. This can be written $\frac{dY}{Y} \Big/ \frac{dX}{X} = \frac{dY}{dX} \cdot \frac{X}{Y}$. However, in the double-log model $\frac{dY}{dX} = \frac{b_1 Y}{X}$. Therefore, elasticity equals

$$b_1 \frac{Y}{X} \frac{X}{Y} = b_1.$$

[5]"Oldest brother" is not necessarily older than respondent but is the oldest brother that respondent has, although he must be at least 21 years old or married in order to be counted.

[6]My dissertation, on which this monograph is based, contains a detailed comparison of the differences in the elasticities obtained by including and excluding people in the "same city" category in the regressions. The only major difference is that the elasticities are increased when people in the "same city" category are omitted.

[7]Bott (1957:143), Adams (1968:129), Mogey (1956:78) and Young and Willmott (1957:59) all discuss this possibility. Aiken finds (1964:87-92) that if either wife's or husband's mother is alive, frequency of visiting both primary and secondary relatives increases.

[8]Litwak and Szelenyi (1969), for example, suggest that kin, friends, and neighbors perform different functions for the individual.

CHAPTER 3

OCCUPATIONAL STATUS, MOBILITY AND PARENTAL CONTACT

Introduction

Socioeconomic status and mobility are usually assumed to influence contact between kin, although theorists differ considerably in their views on both the reasons for and the direction of their impact. Because of the importance of these factors in the literature on kinship some of the hypotheses which have been put forward will be scrutinized to see which, if any, are supported by the available data.

Part I. Socioeconomic Status and Parental Contact

Why should socioeconomic status affect the contact of adult children with their family of orientation? There are several answers, depending on how socioeconomic status is operationalized. Even though the discussion is limited to the effect of occupational status, as it is in most empirical research, and as I propose to limit it, occupational differences are assumed to represent a variety of underlying factors and therefore, occupational status is hypothesized to exert a variety of effects.

To some sociologists, occupational differences represent class, therefore cultural differences which determine the importance attached to the extended family and to the maintenance of contact with the family of orientation; for example, Hollingshead and Redlich (1958, Chapter 4). Those who adopt this view usually assume that working-class families (and very upper-class families) are more family-oriented or more closely knit than middle-class families, as do, for example, Willmott and Young in their studies in England (1957 and 1960). Although research oriented toward description of cultural variation usually consists of case studies and therefore lacks a comparative base (except insofar as the findings of one study can be compared with those of another) the assumption that working-class families are more family-oriented is not based solely on observation. It is usually supported by specification of the functions which these families perform for one another.

One such function is the provision of economic help, and particularly help in finding jobs and housing, as is documented by Bott (1957:122), Garigue (1956:1097) and Young and Willmott (1957:73). There is no reason why this would not occur in middle-class families, too; in fact, Sussman (1959:336) reports that middle-class families are more likely to give and receive financial aid than are working-class families; and Sharp and Axelrod (1956:437) find no income differences in the giving and receiving of various kinds of help within the family. Nevertheless, it is possible that direct assistance from the members of the family in finding jobs and help in occupational performance itself is possible only in certain occupations such as farming, unskilled labor, and craft occupations, where parents may be useful in obtaining union membership. Such situations, however, would be unlikely to hold true of more than a small proportion of the population. Most so-called "middle-class" occupations, particularly the professional and technical, depend on education or training, in which the family cannot be directly helpful. That is, help provided by the family must occur at an earlier age and not by way of direct intervention but by way of socialization and support in obtaining an education, and this does not necessitate or stimulate continued contact between adult children and parents.[1] However, proprietors and managers, who are usually classified as in middle-class occupations, may be as likely as working-class parents to provide job opportunities for their children — a place in the family business, for example. Hence greater frequency of contact resulting from occupational help provided by the family cannot safely be used to predict the influence of occupational status.

Another view of occupational differences is as an index of economic differences. Since gradations in occupational status usually correspond to differences in income and other economic resources, and since, as already observed, cost is important in determining frequency of parental contact, this reasoning usually leads to the conclusion that people with "middle-class" or white-collar occupations are more likely to maintain parental contact since they obviously can afford it.[2] But in these usually upper-middle and upper-class families, with property rights and substantial material wealth, there is even more reason for adult children and parents to maintain contact. Another consideration, mentioned by Michel (1960), is that working-class families are less able to control their living conditions, and that, in Paris at least, many working-class families are split up because the housing shortage forced some members to become permanent residents of furnished hotels and made it impossible for extended families to live near one another.

Status or Distance?

It is sometimes argued that the economic advantages of the middle class are counterbalanced by the fact that people of lower occupational status live closer to their parents and therefore can afford to see them more often. This bring up a problem in the existing empirical work on the effects of socioeconomic status on contact. If individuals of lower occupational status do live closer to their parents (and we do not know this to be true), then the effects of status and distance are confounded, and we do not know whether the differences observed in diverse status groups are effects of occupation or of distance. Adams, for example (1968:45), attributes status differences in contact to differences in distance but since he does not include the effects of both simultaneously in a model the two cannot be separated. Aiken's data (1964: 124) on families with parents in the Detroit area show that 87 percent of white-collar respondents and 82 percent of blue-collar respondents see their husbands' parents at least once or twice a week when the parents live in the same neighborhood. The comparable percentages when parents live outside the neighborhood are 61 percent and 42 percent.[3] The fact that the differences are much larger in the case of parents outside the neighborhood suggests that cost may be playing a part in making the visits of blue-collar respondents relatively rare.[4] However, distance may enter into the differences between blue-collar and white-collar respondents in the "outside the same neighborhood" category.

Axelrod (1956), who combines relatives outside the immediate family into a single group, finds no linear relationship between socioeconomic status (as measured by a combined social status scale, income and education) and the percentage who see relatives at least a few times a month. If anything, the pattern is nonmonotonic with individuals of high and low status showing the least contact, and those in the middle the greatest. Axelrod also does not control distance. Stuckert reports that "upper-status persons tend to visit members of their families more frequently than do lower-status persons" (1963:304). However, my own computations from his data show that of husbands who have parents living in the Milwaukee area, 50.2 percent of his upper-status respondents, 37.8 percent of those of middle status, and 44.6 percent of those with lower status make one or more visits a week—results which are hardly unequivocal.

To summarize: neither the theoretical nor the empirical literature leads to any clear-cut expectations about differences in parental contact and occupational status, except insofar as such differences may be correlated with residential proximity. For every argument predicting effects in one direction there is an equally plausible argument predicting effects in the opposite direction. In fact, at least one author (Firth, 1964:84) doubts that there are any class-based differentials in kinship behavior. In the absence of any clear hypotheses, the empirical findings must guide the analysis.

Procedure

In analyzing the effect of occupational status and mobility on contact with kinfolk, I have treated the occupational categories as binary or dummy variables which, for each individual, take on the value of zero if a person is not in the category and of one if he is. The dummy variables are then used in least-squares regression equations to derive coefficients or parameters for the categories in question.[5] For example, if the hypothesis states that there are additive status effects of both son's and father's occupation, given five categories of occupation for each, I would use a model which allowed a separate coefficient for each row and column of Figure 3.1 below.

Since these are the categories which will be used, I have also listed the oc-

Figure 3.1

Father's Occupation by Son's Occupation

		Son's Occupation				
		1	2	3	4	5
	1	1,1	1,2	1,3	1,4	1,5
	2	2,1	2,2	2,3	2,4	2,5
Father's	3	3,1	3,2	3,3	3,4	3,5
Occupation	4	4,1	4,2	4,3	4,4	4,5
	5	5,1	5,2	5,3	5,4	5,5

Notation:

1 — UWC = *Upper White Collar* (including professional, technical, & other such workers; managers, officials, and proprietors, except farm).

2 — LWC = *Lower White Collar* (including sales, clerical and other such workers).

2 — UBC = *Upper Blue Collar* (including craftsmen, foremen, and other such workers).

4 — LBC = *Lower Blue Collar* (including operatives and other such workers; service workers; and laborers, except farm).

5 — *Farm* (including farmers, farm managers, and farm laborers and foremen).

cupational groups included in each. In the additive status model the predicted value of In contact of each individual is the common intercept plus one coefficient for the row of his father's occupation and another for the column of his occupation. Are there then really different effects for each row and column? Another way to ask this question is: is the ability to predict an individual's frequency of contact with kin improved by allowing different coefficients for each row and column? Or would the predictions be just as good if, for example—to use a hypothesis which I will actually test—all non-farmers were treated alike and assigned only two coefficients—one for farmers and one for nonfarmers? This hypothesis may be tested by comparing the variance explained by a model which includes parameters for each row and column to a model which includes only farm and nonfarm parameters. Then, if the former model does not add a significant increment to the explained variance, one is justified in assuming that there are no significant differences among the rows and columns other than the farm-nonfarm difference. In general, the test used to make this comparison is an F-ratio, where

$$F = \frac{(R_1{}^2 - R_2{}^2) \ / \ (k_1 - k_2)}{(1 - R_1{}^2) \ / \ N - k_1 - 1}$$

and R_1^2 = proportion of variance explained by Model 1, which includes all row and column effects.

R_2^2 = proportion of variance explained by Model 2, which includes only farm-nonfarm effect.

k_1 = number of independent variables in Model 1.

k_2 = number of independent variables in Model 2.

N = number of observations.

The value of F obtained can be looked up in a table of F-ratios, with $n_1 = k_1 - k_2$ d.f. and $n_2 = N - k_1 - 1$ d.f.

I have described this procedure in considerable detail because I follow it hereafter when I compare models originating in different substantive hypotheses about the effect of various factors on frequency of contact with kin. It should be kept in mind that the F-tests are used as an aid in judging the magnitude of an effect and in making decisions. They are not meant to indicate statistical significance in the strictest sense, for I cannot always comply with strict statistical assumptions. For example, I sometimes combine categories after looking at the coefficients and then compute a new F-ratio. This procedure cannot be justified statistically, but it helps make sense of the data.

The actual models are often more complicated than the example described above, especially since I plan to consider the possibility that occupational effects are different in people in the "same city" category from what they are in those outside the city of parents' residence. The parameters included in each model will be made clear in the text; however, the actual estimating equations will be given in an appendix, in order to avoid complicating the presentations.

The Effect of Occupational Status

Does occupational status affect parental contact at all? Since the literature implies that occupational status is negatively correlated with residential distance from parents, it is possible, as was suggested earlier, for the effects of distance to have been mistaken for those of occupational status. Therefore, the proper way to test the hypothesized effects of occupational status is to compare the variance explained by a model which includes both them and distance effects with one including distance only. The full model of occupational status used here includes two separate sets of row and column occupational effects, one on those in the same city as parents, the other on those outside, in addition to distance parameters (Equation 1 in Appendix A). The basic distance model includes separate coefficients for people in the same city and those outside (in order to avoid the domination of the regression line by the mean of ln contact of people in the "same city" category) plus a parameter for the effect of the continuous variable, ln distance (Equation 2 in Appendix A). For all people in the same city, ln distance is assumed to be zero, there being no variation in distance among those in this category.

The sample on which this comparison and others in this chapter are based is the sample of husbands used in Chapter I, minus individuals for whom occupation or father's occupation were unknown, which left a total of 374 individuals. The F-ratio used to test the hypothesis stated above on this sample is 2.12, with $n_1 = 16$ and $n_2 = 355$. Since $F_{.05} = 1.71$, which is exceeded by the value obtained, we can assume that there are significant occupational status effects. What these effects are, however, is another question. We gain some clue to them by examining the coefficients in the full occupational status model.

Interpretation of the Coefficients

In working with least-squares regression with dummy variables, it is necessary to introduce a constraint into the equations in order to obtain a solution, since the set of dummy variables for each factor (e.g., the set of five dummy variables for father's occupation) is linearly dependent. That is, if an individual's scores on four of the five dummy variables is known, his score on the fifth can be inferred. For regression purposes the most convenient constraint is to set the coefficient of one of the dummy variables in a set equal to zero by omitting the dummy variable for the appropriate category from the regression equation. The regression coefficients of the remaining categories are then interpreted as deviations from the coefficient of the omitted category, which is zero. As Melichar (1965) points out, this constraint is easy to use, but it sometimes leads to difficulties in interpretation, since it is often not meaningful to eliminate one category rather than another.

An alternative constraint, and the one employed here, is that used in the technique known as multiple classification analysis (MCA). Here the constraint is that the weighted sum of the coefficients for a single factor must equal zero (the weights being the number of individuals in the categories corresponding to each coefficient). The coefficients are then interpreted as deviations from the grand mean of the dependent variable, so that each of the coefficients in Table 3.1 can be interpreted as a deviation from the grand mean of ln contact. The coefficients obtained from the regression equation using the first constraint can be transformed into the coefficients that would be obtained by using the second constraint.[6] As Melichar says also:

> It is worth emphasizing that the results obtained with the two constraints are identical even though the actual values of the coefficents themselves are different. This is because the results of interest are the differences among the coefficients, and these differences are the same regardless of the constraint used.... Identical values are also obtained for the measures of importance and statistical significance.... Thus the only difference between the two methods is the form in which the coefficients are presented to the audience. (1965:375)

In Table 3.1 each respondent's expected frequency of contact starts with the mean ln contact of the total sample. Increments or decrements to the mean are then granted according to the status of the respondent and of his father. In the model used in Table 3.1, these coefficients assigned to a respondent in the same city as the father and to one outside of the father's city are seen to differ. For example, a respondent in an upper white-collar occupaion whose father is a farmer and who lives outside his father's city begins with the mean of ln contact (3.028) and in addition, he is assigned the status coefficient appropriate to him as a husband living outside the father's city: -.162 for being in the upper white-collar category and .074 for having a father who is a farmer. Thus the frequency of contact predicted for him on the basis of his unique membership in status categories is $3.028 - .162 + .074 = 2.940$. Not shown in Table 3.1 but also included in the model are separate coef-

TABLE 3.1

Status Coefficients (using Multiple Classification Analysis
Convention) for Complete Occupational Status Model
of Ln Parental Contact, with Separate Status Effects
on Husbands in "Same City" and "Outside City" Categories

	Coefficients for Husbands in Same City as Father		Coefficients for Husbands Outside City of Father	
	Husband's Occupation	Father's Occupation	Husband's Occupation	Father's Occupation
UWC	-.834	-.203	-.162	.153
LWC	-.384	.120	.181	-.205
UBC	-.595	.337	-.384	-.494
LBC	-.317	-.170	-.170	.121
Farm	.414	-.006	.206	.074
		Mean Ln Contact $= 3.028$		

ficients for the respondent in the same city as father or outside father's city
and a parameter for ln distance as a continuous variable.[7]

One should keep in mind that differences between coefficients are important, not the coefficients themselves. The coefficients are expressed in logarithms to the base e.[8] Thus the difference between the coefficients for upper
white-collar husbands (-.834) and farm husbands (.414) in the same city equals
$-1.248 = \ln b_{UWC} - \ln b_{Farm} = \ln (b_{UWC}/b_{Farm})$. Then b_{UWC}/b_{Farm}
$= e^{-1.248} < 1/3$. This means that farm husbands in the same city contact parents more than three times as often as upper white-collar husbands
in the same city. Some examples of differences in coefficients and the ratios
of contacts to which they correspond are shown in Table 3.2, since they may
be useful in interpreting the coefficients. This table shows, for example, that
if the difference between the coefficients for two groups is 0.0, the frequency
of their contacts is the same, since their ratio is 1.0. If the difference between
coefficients is 1.0, then one group contacts parents over 2.7 times as often as
the other group. A negative difference would correspond to the reciprocal
of the ratio of the positive difference with the same absolute value.

Table 3.1 shows that in the "same city" category the major difference
is that between farm and nonfarm husbands, more contact being found among
farm husbands. The same effect occurs in the "outside city" category; the
differences, however, are much smaller. Effects of father's occupation do not
differ much among themselves in either category, and what differences there
are certainly show no monotonic pattern with occupational status. Neither
do the effects of husband's occupation; however, it is doubtful if these differ
significantly from each other or if the father's occupational differences do,
either), once the farm-nonfarm differences are taken into account. The assumption that the farm-nonfarm differences constitute the only significant

TABLE 3.2

Examples of Differences Between MCA Logarithmic Coefficients
and Corresponding Contact Ratios

If Difference Between Two Coefficients is:	The Ratio of Contact is:
0.0	1.00
0.2	1.23
0.4	1.49
0.6	1.83
0.8	2.23
1.0	2.72

occupational effects can be tested by comparing the model used in Table 3.1 to a model which includes only parameters for farmers vs. nonfarmers inside and outside the city, together with effects of distance. But is it necessary to assume different effects of occupation on people in the two distance categories? Or would prediction be just as good from a model which combines the occupational effects on both categories (Equation 3 in Appendix A)? The F-test for this comparison (with n_1 = 8 and n_2 = 355) yields a value of 2.30; whereas $F_{.05} \doteq 1.98$. Since the observed value exceeds the value of $F_{.05}$ the conclusion is that separate effects must be allowed in the two distance categories, and I will therefore continue to use models which retain them.

To return to the question of the source of the significant effects of occupational status presented in Table 3.1, it can now be seen whether a farm-nonfarm model can explain as much variance as that explained by the complete model of effects of occupational status used in Table 3.1. The proportion of variance explained by the farm-nonfarm model (Equation 4 in Appendix A) is .6612, while that explained by the complete occupational model is .6833. The difference between the two is just barely significant, since the F-ratio is 1.77, whereas $F_{.05}$ (n_1 = 14; n_2 = 355) is approximately 1.76. If the results of this F-test are accepted then there should be a meaningful impact of occupation on parental contact, other than the farm-nonfarm effect. Before straining the imagination to interpret such effects, however, it might be helpful to recompute the coefficients for the complete model of occupational status without including farmers. This allows another test of the hypothesis that the farm-nonfarm effect is the only significant effect of occupation; for if an F-test computed on the model without farmers proves to be nonsignificant and if there are no interpretable differences in the table, then it can be concluded that there are no further effects of occupational status worth interpreting. On the other hand, it is possible that status effects which do exist have gone unobserved in Table 3.1 because of the overriding importance of the farm-nonfarm effect; if so, they should be brought to light by eliminating the farmers from the analysis.

In recomputing the complete model of the effects of occupational status, I used a model which allows four occupational categories for husband's occupation and five for husband's father's occupation, since respondents with farm backgrounds were retained in the sample. I first tested to see whether it was necessary to include separate sets of coefficients for the two distance categories (Equations 5 and 6 in Appendix A) and obtained an F-ratio of 2.48. Since $F_{.05}$ $(n_1 = 7; n_2 = 336) \doteq 2.05$, I did not combine the distance categories, for the difference between the models is significant. However, the coefficients themselves in the model which retains separate effects in the two distance categories show that the differences within each set of coefficients are small (the largest difference is .653, for the father's occupation coefficients in the "outside city" category), and they fall into no clear pattern.

TABLE 3.3

Status Coefficients (using MCA Convention) for Nonfarm Occupational
Status Model of Ln Parental Contact, with Separate Status
Effects for "Same City" and "Outside City" Categories

| | Coefficients for Husbands in Same City as Father | | Coefficients for Husbands Outside City of Father | |
	Husband's Occupation	Father's Occupation	Husband's Occupation	Father's Occupation
UWC	-.418	-.203	.017	.176
LWC	.032	.120	.375	-.205
UBC	-.179	.337	-.197	-.477
LBC	099	-.171	.019	.136
Farm	—	-.006	—	.069
	Mean Ln Contact = 2.951			

If this model is compared to a model which includes only parameters for distance (Equation 2 in Appendix A), the difference between the variance explained by these models is found to be not significant, since the F-ratio is 1.72, while $F_{.05}$ $(n_1 = 14; n_2 = 332) \doteq 1.76$. If therefore seems safe to conclude that differences in neither present occupational status nor in status of origin affect how frequently married males visit their fathers.

In the models on which the coefficients in Tables 3.1 and 3.2 are based, distance was included in order to avoid confounding possible effects of status with effects of distance. It is sometimes argued that lower- and working-class people live closer to their parents and visit them oftener for that reason. By including distance in the models I have effectively ruled out any differences in contact which are due to underlying differences in distance between the occupational categories. What is surprising, however, is to find that even if distance is *not* controlled, there is still no clear pattern of differences in contact by status. In a model which is exactly the same as that used in Table

3.1 except for the exclusion of ln distance, the coefficients for husbands out-side the city of father are as follows: UWC (-.835), LWC (.196), UBC (-.715), LBC (-.525), and Farm (.625). (The coefficients for those in the same city as father remain the same as those in Table 3.1, since distance in the case of respondents in this category was originally uncontrolled.) The differences be-tween coefficients are larger than those in Table 3.1, where distance was controlled. However, the farmers still are the ones who keep up the most frequent contact, followed by lower white-collar workers. Contrary to expecta-tion, neither blue-collar category of respondents shows frequent contact, as would be the case if they lived closer to parents. Thus, not only are there no direct effects of occupation other than the farm-nonfarm effect, but there is also no predictable pattern of indirect effects operating through distance.

Farm vs. Nonfarm Differences

Since the farm-nonfarm differences are the only significant occupational effects on parental contact, it would be worthwhile to examine these dif-ferences more closely. Table 3.4 shows the coefficients added to or subtracted from an individual's score for a farm or a nonfarm occupation and for being inside or outside father's city.

TABLE 3.4

Farm and Nonfarm MCA Coefficients for Farm-Nonfarm Model of Ln Parental Contact, with Separate Farm Coefficients for "Same City" and "Outside City" Categories

	Coefficients for Husbands in Same City as Father	Coefficients for Husbands Outside City of Father
Farm	.408	.289
Nonfarm	-.523	-.283
	Mean Ln Contact = 3.028	

For this model the expected value of ln contact is:

5.230 — to farmers in the city of father's residence.
4.299 — to nonfarmers in the city of father's residence.
$5.926 - .718 \ln D_i$ — to farmers outside the city of father's residence.
$5.354 - .718 \ln D_i$ — to nonfarmers outside the city of father's residence.

These differences are not trivial. For example, the difference between farmers and nonfarmers in the "same city" category, when converted to antilogs, amounts to a difference of approximately 113 contacts per year! Another way to put it is to point out that farmers in the same city are in contact with parents over 2½ times as frequently as nonfarmers living in the same city as parents.

It is obvious from Table 3.4 that the farm-nonfarm difference in the "same city" category is greater than the comparable difference outside the city. However, distance outside the city has been controlled, and it cannot be controlled inside the city. Therefore the large difference inside the city may be due mostly to the fact that farmers who say they live in the "same city" as parents may actually live much closer to parents than nonfarmers who live in the "same city" (for example, in the same household or on adjoining land).9 There is, in fact, a negative correlation between distance from parents and being a farmer among those living outside the city of their parents' residence. This is demonstrated by the reduction in the farm-nonfarm difference which occurs when distance from city of parents is controlled. In a farm-nonfarm model which does not include distance (Equation 7 in Appendix A) the difference between farmers and nonfarmers outside the city was 1.31. This difference is reduced to .572 (= .289--.283) when distance is controlled, as Table 3.4 shows. Thus over half of the observed difference in frequency of contact between farmers and nonfarmers outside the city of parents' residence is explained by the fact that farmers are still likely to live closer to their parents and therefore to have more frequent contact with them.

Not only does this finding indicate the importance of controlling distance when looking at effects of other variables, but it also supports Parsons' argument (1954) that farm families provide an exception to the relatively isolated conjugal pattern characteristic of an industrial and predominantly urban society. Historically, the finding also implies that as the proportion of farmers in the population declines with increasing industrialization, the mean distance between adult children and their parents will increase as a consequence, and contact with parents will be less frequent.

Aside from the effect of distance, are there characteristics of farmers which make them more likely to maintain contact with parents? This question is important especially to those in the "same city" category, but it cannot be solved directly, since within-city distances are not available. It may be approached indirectly by asking whether the farm-nonfarm difference in the "outside city" category is significant. If it is not, then it is plausible to conclude that differences in the "same city" category would also not be significant if distance were controlled; and, therefore, that differences between farmers and nonfarmers are really due to differences in their distance from their parents. To test this hypothesis the model used in Table 3.4 is compared to a model which assumes no farm-nonfarm differences in the "outside city" category and therefore combines farmers and nonfarmers (Equation 8 in Appendix A). The farm-nonfarm difference within the city would be retained, however. The F-ratio is 1.96, whereas $F_{.05} (n_1 = 1; n_2 = 369) \doteq$ 3.89. Therefore the farm-nonfarm difference outside the city does not add a significant increment to the variance explained by a model which includes a farm-nonfarm parameter in the "same city." According to the latter model, the expected value of ln contact is:

5.231   to farmers in the city of father's residence.

4.299   to nonfarmers in the city of father's residence.

$5.412 - .725 \ln D_i$ to anyone (farmer or nonfarmer) outside the city of father's residence.

If there were thought to be something characteristic of farmers other than their distance, it might be more appropriate to use a model which allows simply a farm-nonfarm parameter; that is, a model which combines the farm effects in the two categories of distance (Equation 9 in Appendix A). This model would give expected ln contact values of:

5.086   to farmers in the city of father's residence.

4.310   to nonfarmers in the city of father's residence.

$6.110 - .716 \ln D_i$ to farmers outside the city of father's residence.

$5.334 - .716 \ln D_i$ to nonfarmers outside the city of father's residence.

In this model the difference between farmers and nonfarmers is the same (.776) whether in the "same city" or "outside." The R^2 for this model is .6608, and since it uses the same number of degrees of freedom as the preceding model, which allowed a farm-nonfarm effect only in the "same city" category, we cannot choose between them on statistical grounds. Rather, the choice depends on whether characteristics of farmers, aside from their distance from parents are hypothesized as affecting their contacts with their parents.

The Effect of Farm Background

If there are such differences they might be expected to show among people of farm background. If, for example, farm families retain the traditions of preindustrial societies more than do nonfarm families, including strong attachment to their kinfolk, then some measure of this traditionalism may be perpetuated by their children even though the children are not farmers themselves. Nonfarm husbands with farm backgrounds would then be intermediate between farm husbands and nonfarm husbands with nonfarm backgrounds in the frequency of their contacts. The MCA coefficients for a model which differentiates between these categories (Equation 10 in Appendix A) presented in Table 3.5 turn out to show hardly any difference between nonfarm husbands with farm backgrounds and those with nonfarm backgrounds in either category of distance. The real difference is still between farmers and nonfarmers. This interpretation is confirmed by the fact that including separate parameters for farm background adds no significant increment to the variance explained by the same model except for these parameters (Equation 4 in Appendix A). The F-ratio for this comparison is .38, while $F_{.05} (n_1 = 2; n_2 = 367) \doteq 3.04$. This finding lends further support to the conclusion that differences between farmers and nonfarmers in frequency of contact while real and large, are due to the fact that farmers live closer to their parents than do nonfarmers.

Summary

To summarize the findings thus far: I came to the conclusion that additive effects of occupational status had no influence on parental contact. However, there is a substantial difference between the frequency of contact of farmers and of nonfarmers, one explanation being that farmers live closer to their parents and therefore visit them more easily. This explanation is supported by the fact that when distance is controlled, the difference between farmers and nonfarmers outside the "same city" category is reduced considerably, so that it no longer contributes any predictive power to that offered by a model which assumes a farm-nonfarm difference in contact only in the same city.

TABLE 3.5

Status Coefficients (using MCA Convention) for Farm-Nonfarm
Background—Nonfarm Model of Ln Parental Contact,
with Separate Coefficients for "Same City" and
"Outside City" Categories

	Coefficients for Husbands in Same City as Father	Coefficients for Husbands Outside City of Father
Farm	.408	.288
Nonfarm with Farm Background	-.444	-.145
Nonfarm with Nonfarm Background	-.537	-.318

Mean Ln Contact = 3.028

The latter model is based on the assumption that farm-nonfarm differences in the "same city" category reflect effects of distance which cannot be eliminated because we cannot measure variation in distance in this category.

The conclusion that farmers are in more frequent contact with their parent because of their greater proximity was strengthened by the elimination of the hypothesis that farm-nonfarm differences are attributable to traditions still, presumably, maintained by farmers, including the preserving of strong ties to the family of orientation. If this were so, then we might expect the nonfarm sons of farmers to perpetuate the traditional orientation and to pay more family visits than nonfarmers without farm backgrounds, though fewer than farmers themselves; but no such differences were found. The farm-nonfarm differences cannot therefore be ascribed to tradition. Rather, they derive from the fact that farmers remain closer in physical distance to their parents, a situation which may mean that they cultivate land owned by or obtained from their parents, or more generally, that farming is one of the few remaining occupations where residing near the family of orientation promotes one's occupational interests.

Part II. Occupational Mobility and Parental Coontact

Occupational mobility has been regarded as the cause of many phenomena [10] but the most relevant to our purposes, of course, are its assumed effects on family cohesion and parental contact.

One school of thought hypothesizes that both upward and downward mobility lead to reduced contact with the family of orientation, since mobility in either direction leads to assimilation into new reference groups and new cultural patterns which may discourage interaction with the family of orientation. Proponents of this view include Locke (1940) and LeMasters (1954). Others reach the same conclusion by a different route: they assume that both the upwardly and the downwardly mobile maintain less frequent contact with their parents, but for different reasons. The upwardly mobile may not want to be reminded of their humble origins; Strodtbeck (1958:156), for example, observes that achievers tend to be anti-familistic; and Schneider and Homans (1955:1204) claim that "upward (sic) mobile persons keep only shallow ties with members of their kindred, if they keep them at all." And in the case of the downwardly mobile, it may be the parents, who do not want to be reminded of the failure of their children and, by extension, their own failure. According to Schneider and Homans again, "Downward (sic) mobile persons may be neglected by their kindred." (1955:1204)

These hyptheses are contradicted by others, who assume for any of several reasons that mobility will not reduce parental contact. Litwak (1960), for example, argues that the family offers deference to upwardly mobile children and deference may be necessary if occupational achievement is to seem worthwhile. Bott states that occupational achievements of children are regarded as positive accomplishments of the parents as well, and therefore would not keep parents and offspring apart (Bott, 1957:107).[11] In general, these arguments assume that parents serve as a necessary reference group for upwardly mobile children, a function which would stimulate visiting. Downwardly mobile children, however, may identify themselves with their parents, thereby reducing their sense of personal failure. Furthermore, the family of orientation can also help to raise or maintain the standard of living of downwardly mobile children (Litwak, 1960).

Another possibility is also put forward by Bott (1957:144); namely, that mobility may affect contact only if the differences in status are very great. Such empirical studies as do exist, however, generally find no unique effects of mobility. Litwak (1960), combining various categories of relatives, finds that of individuals with relatives in the same city, the percentage making one or more family visits per week is highest in the "stationary upper" category ("upper" is equivalent to upper white-collar in my data), lowest in the "stationary manual" category ("manual" is equivalent to upper blue-collar and lower blue-collar in my data), and intermediate in the upwardly and downwardly mobile.[12] He also compares those who move two steps up or down (from manual to upper and vice versa) and again finds no effect of mobility.[13] Adams (1968:44) also appears to find none; but since he does not control distance at all, one cannot easily interpret his data.

Empirically the soundest of these studies is that by Aiken and Goldberg, who use multiple classification analysis to predict frequency of contact with husband's parents on the basis of an additive model (that is, a model which posits "middle-class" and "working-class" effects but none of mobility) and who discuss the fit of such an additive model to the actual data. They argue that if mobility reduces contact, then the predicted values of contact using an additive model should be higher than the actual values in the mobile categories. Their data indicate that this is not the case: an additive model appears to describe the data adequately. However, they do not demonstrate that it is even necessary to posit additive effects of status; and in the case of contact with husband's parents, such effects are not obvious from the data. They also do not control distance, except insofar as they do so by analyzing only respondents whose fathers live in the Detroit area. An additional difference between their sample and mine is that there are no farmers in their sample. Nevertheless, their conclusions regarding mobility are virtually the same as my own.

Procedure

The procedure in testing to find if there are effects of mobility is basically the same as that followed earlier in the analysis of effects of occupational status. That is, models which include coefficients for the various mobility effects noted in the literature are compared to a basic model which excludes them, in order to see whether the increment in variance explained by the mobility effects is sufficient to justify assuming their existence. In this part of the analysis, however, the basic model against which comparisons will be made includes both distance and parameters of farm-nonfarm differences in the "same city" category (Equation 8 in Appendix A). The reason for including the latter parameters is that the previous analysis showed that the farm-nonfarm differential was the only significant effect of status (an effect which, I concluded, was really due to distance); and since I do not want this effect to be confounded with possible effects of mobility, I include it in the basic model against which comparisons are made.

A Simple Mobility Model

The first mobility model to be considered is a model which assumes only a single effect of upward and downward mobility, combined (Equation 11 in Appendix A). This model distinguishes between "stable" respondents – those in the diagonal cells of Figure 3.1 (cells $(1,1)$, $(2,2)$, $(3,3)$, $(4,4)$ $(5,5)$) – and "mobile" respondents – those in any of the remaining cells. Again, I use dummy variables to represent stable and mobile individuals and obtain different expected values of ln in contact to the stable and the mobile respondents.

At this point the question arises: Is it necessary to assume different effects of mobility on individuals in the "same city" and "outside city" categories? An F-test of this assumption (comparing Equation 11 to Equation 12 in Appendix A) yields an F-ratio of .87, while $F_{.05}$ $(n_1 = 1; n_2 = 368) \doteq 3.89$. Therefore, it may be assumed that mobility's effects, if they exist, do not differ according to distance, and the effect of mobility may be examined in the sample as a whole. According to the simple mobility model (Equation 12 in Appendix A) the increment added for being mobile is .052, whereas it is -.099 in the case of the stable respondents. However, the difference between the models is not significant, since the F-ratio is only 2.07, whereas $F_{.05}$ $(n_1 = 1; n_2 = 369) \doteq 3.89$. Therefore mobility *per se* cannot be said to have any distinct effect. Furthermore, the coefficient for mobility is positive, rather than negative, as the literature would lead one to expect – that literature which leads to expectation of any effect at all.

Upward vs. Downward Mobility

It is possible that mobility appears to exert no influence because upward and downward mobility have opposite effects which cancel one another when combined. This hypothesis can be tested by allowing separate coefficients for upward and downward mobility and comparing this model (Equation 13 in Appendix A) to the basic model described above (Equation 8 in Appendix A). Again the first test is to see whether it is necessary to allow separate effects of mobility upon the two distance categories (compare Equation 13 to Equation 14 in Appendix A). The F-ratio is 1.12, and $F_{.05}$ (n_1 = 3; n_2 = 365) $\doteq$ 2.65 so the effects of mobility in the two distance categories can be combined. These effects in the combined model (Equation 14 in Appendix A) are:

Upwardly Mobile: .028
  Cells (2,1) (3,1) (3,2) (4,1) (4,2) (4,3) (5,1) (5,2) (5,3) (5,4)
Downwardly Mobile: .105
  Cells (1,2) (1,3) (1,4) (1,5) (2,3) (2,4) (2,5) (3,4) (3,5) (4,5)
Stable: -.099
  Cells (1,1) (2,2) (3,3) (4,4) (5,5)

Again, these effects are not significant, for when compared to the basic model the F-ratio is only 1.69, while $F_{.05}$ (n_1 = 2, n_2 = 366) $\doteq$ 3.04. Both effects are positive as well, which rules out the possiblity that the effect of upward mobility is the opposite of that of downward mobility. In actuality, there is no evidence of either effect.

Extreme Mobility

Although neither upward nor downward mobility affects contact, it may be that, as Bott (1957:144) argues, only large differences in occupational status inhibit it. Within the limits of the data this hypothesis can be tested by defining as extremely mobile those who have moved two or more steps away from their father in occupational status. Thus an intergenerational move from upper blue-collar to upper white-collar status would count as extreme mobility, whereas a move from lower white-collar to upper white-collar would not. Testing first a model which combines extreme upward and extreme downward mobility (Equation 15 in Appendix A) again shows it is unnecessary to consider separately the mobility effects of the two distance categories (F = .22; $F_{.05}$ (n_1 = 1; n_2 = 366) $\doteq$ 3.89) (obtained from Equations 15 and 16 in Appendix A). Combining these categories, as far as mobility effects are concerned, the effect of extreme mobility (which includes cells (3,1), (4,1), (4,2), (5,1), (5,2), (5,3), (1,3), (1,4), (1,5), (2,4), (2,5), and (3,5) in Figure 3.1 becomes .066. The effect of stability (all the remaining cells) is -.034, which is not significant, as the appropriate F-test shows (F = 1.41; $F_{.05}$ (n_1 = 1; n_2 = 369) $\doteq$ 3.89.

Finally, to consider the hypothesis that the effect of extreme upward mobility differs from that of extreme downward mobility (Equation 17 in Appendix A): here again effects in the "same city" and "outside city" categories can be combined (Equation 18 in Appendix A) since the F-test comparing the model with separate coefficients to that with coefficients for the combined sample yields a value of .11, while $F_{.05}$ (n_1 = 2; n_2 = 366) $\doteq$ 3.04. Then the coefficients are:

Extremely Upwardly Mobile: .048
  Cells (3,1) (4,1) (4,2) (5,1) (5,2) (5,3)

Extremely Downwardly Mobile: .109
   Cells (1,3) (1,4) (1,5) (2,4) (2,5) (3,5)
Stable or Not Extremely Mobile: -.034
   All other cells

Once again, the explained variance added by the mobility effects is not significant: the F-ratio is only .77, and $F_{.05}$ (n_1 = 2; n_2 = 368) $\doteq$ 3.04. Thus none of the mobility effects studied here—including simple combined mobility, upward vs. downward mobility, extreme combined mobility, or extreme upward vs. extreme downward mobility—can be shown to affect the contact of married males with their fathers.

Discussion

I have been unable to demonstrate that mobility, as defined in this study, affects parental contact. I have assumed that in order to justify assuming the existence of mobility effects, such effects must explain variance in contact in addition to that already explained by distance (and farm-nonfarm parameters which, I assume, also represent an effect of distance). In a sense, the present research is more hospitable to the possibility of mobility effects than is that of Aiken and Goldberg, for mine does not require mobility effects to compete with an additive model of status effects. However, I had already concluded that there were no additive effects of status, so these additional parameters were unnecessary. Ordinarily, however, mobility effects or any hypothesized interaction effects would be considered only after additive effects were allowed to explain as much variance as possible.

Given the fact that I was consistently unable to reject the null hypothesis of no mobility effects and that my findings support those of other empirical studies, it might be wise if in further research factors other than occupational mobility were investigated. However, certain shortcomings in the present data could preclude the finding of existing mobility effects. Larger samples, for example, would probably include more extreme ranges of variation to test the hypothesis of extreme mobility. Mobility might also affect contact with other relatives more than that with parents.[14] Other kinds of mobility which more directly reflect breaks in cultural tradition or changes in membership in specific groups may also be more promising than changes in occupation.[15] Not only is occupational status a more or less continuous variable, changes in which are unlikely to involve great changes in life style, but an occupation is regarded by many as only a means of making the money to enjoy a life style which is determined by other attributes, such as ethnicity or religion. The impact of intergenerational changes in occupation upon cultural patterns may have been seriously overrated by sociologists and others to whom a profession brings a way of life.

FOOTNOTES

[1] Blau and Duncan (1967) show, in their basic model of the process of stratification in the United States, that about ¼ of the gross effect of father's occupation on son's occupation is direct (p. 170). Even if this direct effect represented factors which are all directly conducive to the maintenance of contact between adult sons and their fathers, three quarters of it is indirect through factors such as education (son's and father's) and son's first job. One would not expect these factors to play any direct part in the maintaining of contact with the parental family.

[2] Litwak (1960) makes this argument. Reiss (1962) also points out that the "time-cost-distance factor" is perceived by many of his respondents as a major determinant of contact between kin.

[3] Aiken's findings (1964) with regard to parents differ from those on relatives as a group. For the latter he does find (using various measures of contact) that contact is more frequent in the working class than in the middle class—which indicates that it is important to analyze the various categories of relatives separately, rather than by combined measures.

[4] Sussman and White (1959:8) point out that nonwhites in their sample in Cleveland were likely to visit out-of-town relatives less frequently than were whites. They attribute this difference to the cost, which prevents nonwhites, with their lower incomes, from visiting oftener. This suggests that the elasticity of visiting with respect to distance, rather than being constant, may be affected by socioeconomic status (or race)—an interaction hypothesis which I will not consider in the present analysis beyond maintaining the separate categories, "same city" and "outside city."

[5] See Suits (1957) for a description of the use of dummy variables in least-squares regression. Also see Melichar (1965) for a description of alternate constraints which can be used to derive a least-squares solution. The constraint used in multiple classification analysis which he discusses is employed later in this chapter.

[6] For the algebraic details of this transformation, see Melichar (1965). See Blau and Duncan (1967:128-140) for another discussion of multiple classification analysis.

[7] If the MCA convention is used, in computing an expected value it is necessary to treat values of continuous independent variables as deviations from their means.

[8] See Hill (1959) for a discussion of the constraints in a multiplicative model corresponding to those in an additive model. In the multiplicative model, made additive by taking the logarithms of the variables, the dummy variables are considered to be exponents of the parameters. The parameters estimated by regression are the logs of the parameters in the original multiplicative equation.

[9] I have no way of knowing what the code "same city" meant in the case of farmers, who do not as a rule live in cities. Therefore, I can only speculate on the differences between farmers and nonfarmers who live in the "same city."

[10] For review of the literature on mobility and discussion of hypotheses regarding its consequences, see Blau (1956) and Janowitz (1956), among others. A recent collection of papers on mobility is that of Smelser and Lipset (1966).

[11] Robins and Tomanec (1962:345) also hold that "Homologies of status do not appear to be very important in deteriming relationships with relatives." Young and Willmott (1957:153) conclude that in the district they studied in East London "social mobility appears to have no marked independent influence except as it promotes geographical mobility."

[12] He eliminates from his sample the stable middle group, farmers and people with farm backgrounds. His measure of contact does not control the differential availability of relatives, which is likely to vary with status.

[13] Stuckert (1963) does indicate the existence of mobility effects. However, he uses the mobility of wives, defined as movement between the occupations of their fathers and their husbands. He then presents data on the percent of husbands and of wives who keep in contact with their own and spouse's family at least once a week. Apparently he uses the wife's status throughout the analysis, so his data for husbands show husbands' contacts as affected by wife's status. In any case, his data show lower percentages in mobile individuals than in stable in each of three status categories. Like Litwak, he combines relatives and does not control their differential availability. He also combines upward and downward mobility.

[14] Garigue (1956) concludes that mobile individuals do not abandon kinship obligations. However, for them kin at or near the status level of destination take the place of kin at the status level of origin.

[15] Aiken and Goldberg (1969) do find evidence that religious mobility (between religions of wife's mother and wife) does depress contact with parents. Garigue (1956) observes that in French Canada marriage with non-French-Canadians reduces contacts with genealogically distant relatives but not with parents.

CHAPTER 4

ADDITIONAL VARIABLES
AND PARENTAL CONTACT

Introduction

This chapter carries on the analysis of the effects on parental contact of several additional variables. The latter fall naturally into three groups: (1) ethnicity and religion, (2) city size and region. (3) age of husband and parent. The findings are presented in the first three parts of this chapter.

Although all these variables have been considered in the literature in relation to family cohesion in general, or to kin contact in particular, the discussion is often very limited and empirical evidence is usually completely lacking. For that reason the present analysis must be considered as exploratory. I therefore examine the effects of each variable separately in models which exclude and include distance. However, the greatest emphasis is placed on the variables which appear to affect parental contact directly; that is, whose effects still remain when distance is included. Only such variables are included in the models presented in Part IV, which goes into the question whether the effects observed in the preceding sections remain when all other variables affecting contact are also included in the model.[1]

Part I. Ethnicity and Religion

Ethnic differences in contact with kin are little more than an untested possibility, despite widespread theoretical interest in ethnic differences in family cohesion and numerous case studies of particular ethnic groups. While the case studies do not lead to predictions about differences between specific ethnic groups, they do raise questions which can be tentatively examined in the light of the present data.

Two broad characterizations of family structure occur repeatedly in the literature on ethnic minorities, ethnic enclaves, and ethnic subcommunities. To some extent the two are contradictory; however, they often appear in the same study and are sometimes used to describe subgroups within an ethnic category. One characterization is in terms of the patriarchal tradition in the homeland and its persistence in immigrant ethnic groups. Child (1943:28), Firey (1947:184), and Campisi (1948:443-449), for example, stress the strong family organization of Italians in the United States. Others, often the same writers, while assuming the patriarchal traditional of ethnic groups before emigration, interpret it as originating in conditions of existence in the primarily agricultural homeland and no longer functional or viable after immigration. Warner and Srole (1945:102), for example, say

> The patriarchal type of family structure was not merely enforced by tradition but took its form in every case except that of the Jews from its functions in a relatively simple agrarian economy.

Many reasons are cited for the breakdown of strong family organization among immigrants, including differential assimilation of the members of the family, demonstrated often in differences in ability to learn the new language.[2] Here children have an advantage, since they learn English in school, while their parents, lagging behind them in mastering English and unable to cope with the intricacies of a foreign culture, lose contact with them. Lack of economic opportunity for the father and the more numerous job openings for the mother also cause the father to lose his traditional place as head of the family, as is documented, for example, in Glazer and Moynihan's discussion of Puerto Ricans (1963:126) and Humphrey's description of Mexicans (1944). This argument is applied particuarly to the case of nonwhites, including Negroes, Puerto Ricans, and Mexicans.

There is a difference, however, between the arguments applied to immigrant groups and those applied to nonwhites. In the case of the former, intergenerational discontinuity and disorganization are often regarded as occurring between the first and second generations in this country. For example, Child (1943) classifies second-generation Italians into those rebelling against the Italian traditions of the first generation, those accepting them, and the apathetic. Others may not have described such neatly and arbitrarily divided categories; however, they point out the discontinuity between the first and the second generation. In the case of nonwhites, it is usually assumed that family disorganization is perpetuated from generation to generation, either because the conditions (e.g., economic disadvantage) which give rise to it are faced anew by each generation, or because the family disorganization of one generation becomes self-perpetuating through the process of socialiation.[3]

In the studies mentioned, Italians, Negroes, and Puerto Ricans in the United States have received most of the attention, reflecting the dominant interest of sociologists specializing in the analysis of ethnic differences. The literature on other minorities is sparse, perhaps because it is assumed that they are no longer characterized by ethnic traditions. For example, in discussing the Irish in New York, Glazer and Moynihan argue that Irish identity is declining in America, and that "it now identifies someone as plain as against fancy American" (1963:250). Thomas (1956:108) comments that the Irish and German Catholics of the Old Immigration have become assimilated and display few specifically ethnic traits. The same would undoubtedly be even more true of the English, Scottish, and other Northwest Europeans.

Following the implications of the literature, ethnic differences in parental contact may take two major directions. If groups of more recent immigration are characterized by a strong family tradition, compared to those of earlier periods of immigration—that is, if there has been cultural continuity of their traditions—then Southern and Eastern Europeans would be expected to maintain more frequent contact with their parents than Northern and Western Europeans. However, if the former suffered from family disorganization and intergenerational discontinuity in the past, then they might be slow in regaining the stable family structure which characterizes the latter. In this case the earlier immigrants would show higher rates of contact, not because of their particular cultural traditions, but simply because they have overcome or never experienced the disorganizing conditions which beset the later immigrants. These alternative hypotheses should be borne in mind in the examination of ethnic differences in the frequency of contact between husbands and their parents.

Procedures and Findings

Ethnic identification of the respondents in the basic sample of husbands was established by asking: "Please tell me what country most of your ancestors came from?" Farmers were eliminated together with all respondents for whom data on any of the variables being studied were missing, the reason being that, in their contacts with their fathers, only they showed the effect of occupational status, (which may have been an effect of distance). If the farmers are eliminated, the analysis of other variables can be carried on without the risk that effects really due to occupational status may be attributed to other variables—unless, of course, status effects have been suppressed by other variables. The possibility that the effects of other variables on contact differ as between farmers and nonfarmers is also ruled out. The remaining sample includes 310 individuals. These were divided into seven ethnic groups (the total number from each nationality being shown in parentheses), as follows:

Austrian (1), Czechoslovakian (1), Hungarian (2), Lithuanian (2), Polish (12), Russian (6), Other Eastern European (4). N = 28

English, Welsh, Canadian, Australian (56), Scottish (12), U.S.A. White (29). N = 97

French (10), Italian (17), Spanish (1). N = 28

German (58), Dutch (7), Swiss (2). N = 67

Irish. N = 23

Mexican (5), Puerto Rican (3), French Canadian (2), U.S. Negro (20), Other Western European (3), Other Asian (3), Other of Western Hemisphere (5), N = 41

Danish (2), Finnish (1), Norwegian (9), Swedish (14). N = 26

Will separate coefficients be necessary for respondents in the city and those outside the city of father's residence? To find the answer, the variance explained by a model with separate coefficients is compared with one which combines the two distance categories in obtaining coefficients for ethnicity

(Equations 1 and 2 in Appendix B). The increment in variance explained by splitting the sample is not significant, since $F = .28$; $F_{.05}$ ($n_1 = 6$; $n_2 = 295$) $\doteq 2.14$. Therefore, it can be assumed that the ethnicity coefficients do not differ in the two distance categories, and the model which includes only one set of coefficients for ethnicity can be used.

Table 4.1 shows the MCA coefficients for ethnicity. In column 1, the coefficients were obtained without including distance in the model (Equation 3 in Appendix B), whereas column 2 shows the comparable coefficients when distance is included (Equation 2 in Appendix B). By comparing these sets of coefficients, we can see how much of the difference in parental contact as between ethnic groups is due to differences in distance. The coefficients are ordered by decreasing magnitude in column 2.

TABLE 4.1

Ethnicity Coefficients (Using MCA Convention) for Ethnicity Models of Parental Contact, Excluding and Including Distance

Ethnicity	Excluding Distance	Including Distance
Irish	1.072	.549
Scandinavian	.222	.523
Eastern European	-.194	.108
French, Spanish, Italian	.780	.023
English, Scottish, U.S.A. White	-.190	-.062
German, Dutch, Swiss	-.233	-.173
Nonwhite and Other	-.313	-.300

Mean Ln Contact = 2.790

By comparing columns 1 and 2 the differences between ethnic groups are seen to be considerably reduced when distance is controlled: the coefficients, which ranged from 1.072 to -.313 in column 1, now range from .549 to -.300. The appropriate F-test comparing the model whose coefficients are shown in column 2 to a model including distance only (Equations 2 and 4 in Appendix B) yields a value of 2.29. Since $F_{.05}$ ($n_1 = 6$; $n_2 = 301$) $\doteq 2.14$, we conclude that these differences are significant (although the differences could be due to factors other than ethnicity which are confounded with ethnic differences.)

The coefficients in column 2 of Table 1 indicate that the Irish and Scandinavians keep up the most frequent contact with their parents and the nonwhites and others the least. The data certainly do not support the idea that Eastern and Southern European husbands are oftener in contact with their fathers due to their strong family traditions. If anything, the data indicate that in groups which are more likely to be assimilated family structures are more stable and therefore more parental contact is maintained—more parental contact than among nonwhites, at least. This interpretation, however, is weakened by the fact that the English, Scottish, and American whites, who ought to be the most assimilated of any group, are not particularly given to frequent parental contact. It is possible that the Irish and Scandinavians are characterized by particularly strong family ties, although one is certainly not led to believe so by the literature on ethnic variation.[4] On the other hand, it is equally possible that the ethnic effects, although statistically significant as a group, are merely the products of the idiosyncrasy of this particular sample and would not occur again in other samples. Only further research can confirm or refute the findings.

Possibly ethnic variation is correlated with some other variable(s), which, if included in the model, would explain the variation which I just now explained by ethnicity. Among rival explanations, religion is one of the first variables which comes to mind. It is possible, for example, that the Irish keep in such frequent contact with their fathers because they are Catholic. Not only are not all Irishmen Catholics, however, but this argument would not account for the frequent kin contact of Scandinavians or the less frequent contact of Italians, French, and Spanish, all of whom come originally from Catholic countries.

Religion and Parental Contact

The literature which leads to the expectation of religious differences in parental contact usually hypothesizes that Catholics and Jews (see Brav, 1940, for an example on Jews) have more closely-knit families than Protestants and presumably keep in closer touch with parents for that reason. Lenski (1963) bases on assumption of this kind on Weber's argument that ascetic Protestantism broke the ties of the extended kin group, thereby allowing social relations on the basis of function. Catholicism, on the other hand, has always promoted strong family structures, and the Catholic family and the Catholic faith support each other.

Looking at empirical evidence, Winch, Greer and Blumberg (1967) find that in an upper middle-class suburb the Jewish household is more likely than the Catholic or the Protestant to have at least twelve households of kin in the metropolitan area with at least five of which it regularly interacts. On these two measures, Catholics were second and Protestants third. As to the Jewish family, in an area where 76 percent of the households sampled turn out to be Jewish, their finding is not surprising. Such an area probably attracts Jews who already have relatives there and who, presumably, are more kinship-oriented than the Jews in a random sample of the total population. Lenski (1963) finds that Jews are the most likely to report weekly visits with relatives, white Catholics are second, white Protestants are third, and Negro Protestants are fourth. However, Lenski points out that Jews and Catholics are also least likely to have migrated to Detroit, where his sample was obtained, and are therefore more likely to have relatives in the Detroit area. Without controls on distance from relatives we cannot interpret the importance of religion as a factor of kin contact.

An alternative hypothesis is that there are no significant religious differences in parental contact. If, as Herberg (1960, Ch. 3) argues, church participation serves as a source of social identification, and if belonging to a church is equivalent to, that is, serves the same functions as belonging to any other voluntary organization (Wilson, 1968; Goode, 1966), then religious differences may be important only because there *are* such differences—in other words, simply because religion allows social identification on another basis besides sex, age, occupation, etc., and not because of any ideological or cultural distinctions inherent in it. If this is true, then we would not expect religious differences to be predictive of cultural differences in kinship obligations, if such do indeed exist.[5] Furthermore, some authors point to ethnic differentiation within religion, particularly the ethnic organization of the Catholic church (Thomas, 1956, Ch. 4; Warner and Srole, 1945, Ch. 7). Even Herberg, who stresses the primacy of the tripartite religious categorization (Catholic, Protestant, Jew) over ethnic categories as sources of social identification, remarks (1960:34):

> The religious community is fast becoming, if it has not already become, the over-all medium in terms of which remaining ethnic concerns are preserved, redefined, and given appropriate expression.

If churches are internally differentiated by ethnicity, and if ethnicity is preserved through the church, then a religious category, such as Catholicism may merely obscure real ethnic differences in family cohesion. If this is the case, then kin contact should be affected more by ethnic than by religious differences. Thus any observed religious differences in parental contact will be eliminated, once ethnicity is included in the model.

One piece of empirical evidence on religion and kin contact is offered by Aiken (1964:145 ff.) who, using wife's religion to characterize the household, finds no significant difference between Protestants, Catholics and Jews in either total amount of contact with kin households in the Detroit area or in average amount of contact with each kin household.[6] This, of course, supports the null hypothesis; however, Aiken does not separate parents from other primary relatives in his analysis. The present data, with more detailed religious categories than his and with distance included in the model, show much the same results.

Procedures and Findings.

The religious categories in my data are:
Baptist N = 69
Episcopalian (11), Presbyterian (13), Lutheran (23). N = 47
Jewish (7), Other (8), None (14). N = 29
Methodist (41), Congregational (5). N = 46
Other Protestant N = 48
Roman Catholic N = 71

Little interpretation can be given to the category, Jewish, Other, None, since there are so few Jews in the sample; but in any case the differences are all so small, once distance is controlled, that it does not stand out from the others. An F-test for the increment added to the explained variance by computing separate coefficients for religious groups in the "same city" and "outside city" categories (comparing Equations 5 and 6 in Appendix B) indicates that this geographical separation is not necessary. $F = 1.07$; $F_{.05}$ ($n_1 = 5$, $n_2 = 296$) $\doteq 2.26$. We can therefore use the coefficients computed for the combined sample. Table 4.2 shows the coefficients for the various religious categories obtained from dummy variable regression. In column 1 the coefficients are shown from a model which does not include distance (Equation 7 in Appendix B); in column 2 they are shown in decreasing order for the model which does include distance (Equation 6 in Appendix B).

TABLE 4.2

Religion Coefficients (Using MCA Convention) for Religion Models of Parental Contact, Excluding and Including Distance

Religion	Excluding Distance	Including Distance
Episcopalian, Presbyterian, Lutheran	.156	.240
Roman Catholic	.432	.065
Other Protestant	.023	.010
Baptist	-.162	.009
Jewish, Other, None	-.600	-.140
Methodist, Congregational	-.230	-.281

Mean Ln Contact = 2.790

When distance is not controlled by inclusion in the model, it is clear that Catholics do maintain somewhat more frequent contact with parents than do any of the others. Within the Protestant denominations, however, there are also gradations, although we cannot say whether the difference between any particular two of them is significant. The Jewish, Other, and None group shows the least contact. However, any speculation about it is risky, as pointed out above, because of its mixed nature.

All these observed differences reflect the fact that members of certain of the religious groups—Catholics, in particular—live closer to their relatives than the others do. Thus their more frequent contacts are due especially in Catholic families to this difference in distance, not to greater cohesion (unless cohesion is defined as living close to parents), since there are no longer any significant differences by religion, if distance is included. An F-test comparing the model represented in column 2 of Table 4.2 to a model including distance only yields a value of .96, while $F_{.05}$ $(n_1 = 5, n_2 = 302) \doteq 2.26$.

Comparison of Ethnicity and Religion

Since there are no significant religious differences left, once distance is included as an explanatory variable, it is unlikely that religion can explain any of the ethnic variation in parental contact. However, the possibility can be verified empirically by including religion, ethnicity, and distance in the same model (Equation 8 in Appendix B). The coefficients for this model are presented in Table 4.3. The ethnicity coefficients are almost identical with those obtained in the earlier model without religion (Table 4.1, column 2), thus demonstrating that religion does not explain the differences in ethnic groups.

TABLE 4.3

Ethnicity and Religion Coefficients (Using MCA Convention) for Ethnicity, Religion, and Distance Model of Parental Contact

Ethnicity Coefficients		Religion Coefficients	
Irish	.581	Episcopalian, Presbyterian Lutheran	.182
Scandinavian	.472	Roman Catholic	.075
Eastern European	.153	Baptist	.069
French, Spanish, Italian	.010	Other Protestant	-.022
English, Scottish, U.S.A. White	-.066	Jewish, Other, None	-.177
German, Dutch, Swiss	-.182	Methodist, Congregational	-.271
Nonwhite and Other	-.283		

Mean Ln Contact = 2.790

The religion coefficients are also similar to those given previously (Table 4.2, column 2). However, they were not significant before, and since their range has been reduced slightly, they certainly are not so now. It can also be demonstrated by F-tests that the contribution of ethnicity remains statistically significant even when religion is in the model, but the contribution of religion remains without significance whether ethnicity is included or not. The relative importance of ethnicity and religion is demonstrated by the fact that ethnicity contributes an additional 1.57 percent to the variance explained by a model which includes only religion and distance, while religion contributes only an additional .51 percent to a model which includes ethnicity and distance.

Summary

Some ethnic variation in parental contact cannot be explained either by distance or by religious differences. The differences refute the theory that immigrants of the more recent periods of immigration have retained the strong family structure characteristic of them in their homelands. Rather, there is some slight indication that the more assimilated, particularly the Irish and Scandinavians, keep most in contact with their parents, especially in comparison with nonwhites and others. Possible explanations are that the former have had a longer time to develop stable family structures in this country and/

or that their families have not been disorganized by economic and social discrimination — explanations which are highly tentative but nevertheless provocative. The findings, of course, could be peculiar to the particular sample I used, or they could indicate real differences in different ethnic groups.

Alternatively, other factors differentially distributed by ethnicity, may explain the differences. Religion, for one, has no effect on parental contact, once differences in distance are taken into account. That Catholics are found to visit their parents oftener, if distance is ignored, is because they live closer to parents than others do. Any explanation of the differences between religious groups, then, must account for the fact that Catholics live closer to their parents. This may be explained by actual differences in religion. Thus members of more traditional churches may be bound by tradition to remain geographically close to their families and so may be less likely to move away as a rational response to occupational self-interest. But, whatever the explanation, the differences in distance must be explained, since distance cancels the effect of the observed religious differences.

Part II. City Size and Region

City Size and Parental Contact

The size of the city is often used as an indicator of urbanization, and hypotheses about the effects of urbanization are sometimes based on effects associated directly with size, at other times on variables related to increasing size, such as the decline in the proportion of the population engaged in agriculture.[7] Since I have eliminated all farm-employed individuals from the sample, effects of city size cannot be attributed to the characteristics associated with an agricultural population. Thus increasing city size and characteristics assumed to be associated with it, rather than more general conceptions of urban-rural differences, are more promising as factors affecting contact with kin.

Wirth (1938) argues that the increasing size of cities leads to greater diversity in their residents, which, in turn, is accompanied by a decline in the importance of primary relationships as forms of social control and cohesion. This has often been interpreted to imply that kinfolk will be less important in an absolute sense; for example, that they will lose their significance as a source of satisfaction or companionship. However, Wirth is primarily concerned with the relative importance of kinship, friendship, and other informal ties, as opposed to formal mechanisms of social control; his argument relates to the functional importance of kinship ties to society as a whole, not to individuals.

Nevertheless, many sociologists have deomonstrated that family ties remain important in urban areas or in urbanized societies. Sussman, for example, states that "kin ties, particularly intergenerational ones, have far more significance than we have been led to believe in the life process of the urban family" (1959:339). Bell and Boat (1957:395) stress the importance in urban neighborhoods of the kin group as a source of informal relations. Aldous (1962) indicates that the extended kinship system still exists in West African cities, and Williamson (1962) shows that family ties serve important functions to individuals in two Central American cities. None of these studies, however, bases its conclusions regarding the relationship between urbanization and kinship ties on comparative data from areas more or less urbanized, regardless of how urbanization is defined. They therefore do not offer much help in explaining why the size of the city, as only one dimension of urbanization, should affect contact with kin.

One possibility is that parental contact is more infrequent in larger cities because of the greater prevalence of disorganized families in larger cities. For example, the nonwhites in the North are likely to live in the larger cities and, as has already been shown, are characterized by lower rates of parental contact. However, effects of this kind are due to ethnicity or race, and even if they appear to be effects of the city's size, they should disappear as soon as the proper explanatory variables are included in the model.

An alternative hypothesis is that there is more family contact in larger cities precisely because of the greater anonymity and impersonality. For example, Sussman and Burchinal (1962:237) conclude that "the difficulty in developing satisfactory primary relationships outside the extended family makes the family in urban areas *more important* to the individual."

Still another possibility is that the size of the city, if it influences kin contact at all, does so only by affecting the distance, or more generally the cost, especially in time, involved in visiting relatives. One may extrapolate from evidence presented by Ogburn and Duncan (1964:134) that the distance from home to place of work increases with city size, and more closely with the radius of the city's area; but the analogy between the journey to work and that to visit kin may not be valid. Families may, for example, live in enclaves within the city, in which case there would be no reason to expect the distance from their kin to increase with city size. However, even though the actual distance involved may be the same as in rural areas and in cities of various magnitudes, the many obstacles to transportation in large, densely populated cities may limit the accessibility of relatives. On the other hand, public transportation is usually either nonexistent or inconvenient in small towns and rural areas, offsetting any advantages of low density. Thus an argument about the cost in terms of distance, time, and money of visiting kinfolk in large, in contrast to small, cities is inconclusvie.

Which, if any, of all these hypotheses are supported and which eliminated?

Procedures and Findings

In the present analysis four dummy variables represent the following categories of city size:

Standard Metroplitan Areas (SMA's) of 2,000,000 or more, N = 70
SMA's of 50,000 - 2,000,000, N = 151
Cities and Towns 10,000 - 50,000, N = 40
Counties with No Towns as Large as 10,000, N = 49

First, the test to see whether it is necessary to allow separate coefficients for people in the "same city" and "outside city" categories (Equations 9 and 10 in Appendix B), with distance controlled in both models, brings the finding that the appropriate F-test yields a value of .38, whereas $F_{.05}$ (n_1 = 3, n_2 = 301) $\doteq$ 2.65. Therefore, the distance categories may be combined in examining the coefficients for city size. These coefficients, for models excluding and including distance (Equations 11 and 10 in Appendix B) are presented in Table 4.4.

TABLE 4.4

City Size Coefficients (Using MCA Convention) for City Size Models
of Parental Contact, Excluding and Including Distance

City Size	Excluding Distance	Including Distance
SMA 2,000,000+	-.366	-.004
SMA 50,000-2,000,000	.017	-.112
Cities and Towns 10,000-50,000	-.253	.009
Counties with no Towns as Large as 10,000	.678	.345

Mean Ln Contact = 2.790

It is apparent from the comparison of columns 1 and 2 in Table 4.4 that there is a large difference between the frequency of contact in the smallest category (counties with no towns as large as 10,000) and that in the other categories. However, this difference is due, in large part, to the fact that residents of the smallest places live closer to their parents. In fact, once distance is included in the model, the differences remaining (column 2) are no longer significant. The F-test for a comparison of this model to a model including distance yields a value of only 1.68, whereas $F_{.05}$ $(n_1 = 3, n_2 = 304) \doteq$ 2.65. Even the differences that remain when distance is included may well be due to the uncontrolled differences in distance in the same city, where the variation in distance is not measured. This is suggested by the fact that in a model which retained separate coefficients for city size, the differences between the smallest places and each of the larger were -.316, -.294, and -.276 among respondents outside the city; while those among respondents in the same city were -.357, -.634, and -.434. In other words, the same-city category is contributing more than its share to the differences found in the combined model, and differences in the same city are probably due partly to differences in distance within the city, since the latter have not been eliminated. The effect of city size, either with or without distance, is also nonmonotonic. When distance is included, the second-largest category of city size has the lowest rate of parental contact. Thus, even if the observed differences were significant, they could not be attributed to a monotonic effect of city size. If anything, the findings suggest a distinction between counties with no towns as large as 10,000 and all larger cities. However, none of these differences is large enough to justify further speculation on the effects of city size. On the basis of the data presented here it can only be concluded that the greater frequency with which rural (nonfarm) and small town individuals contact their parents is thanks to their living closer together.

Regional Effects on Parental Contact

Sociologists who speculate on possible regional differences in family cohesion usually begin with causal variables correlated with religion—i.e., more likely to be found in certain regions than others, but not inherent characteristics of regional variation itself. In fact, it is unlikely that regions could have any bearing upon individual behavior except insofar as their composition varies as to other variables. Such differences as are assumed to exist between regions in regard to family cohesion are, in fact, usually attributed to variation in occupational, religious or other circumstances. For example, Blumberg and Bell (1959:332) remark, "It is in many parts of the South that one still finds the most substantial number of persons living in rural farm areas and hence a pool of persons with strong familistic values."[8] It is true that farmers do maintain relatively more frequent contact with parents, as do also residents of rural areas and small towns. However, in either case, the possibility cannot be ruled out that the differences are actually due to differences in distance; that is, that farmers and rural or small-town people live closer to their parents, a fact which may be due to their stronger familistic values, or other causes. In any case, if distance is the cause, then once distance is included any such variation is explained, and there is no reason to hypothesize further regional (in this case, Southern) effects, except those found equally spurious, once the true causal variables are included in the model. Therefore, the null hypothesis seems to be the only plausible one, unless there are true sources of regional variation which are not apparent and which might affect contact with parents.

Procedures and Findings

The regions used in the anlaysis are:

Northeast, N = 71

Maine, New Hampshire, Vermont, Massachusetts, Rhode Island, Connecticut, New York, New Jersey, Pennsylvania

North Central, N = 103

Ohio, Indiana, Illinois, Michigan, Wisconsin, Minnesota, Iowa, Missouri, North Dakota, South Dakota, Nebraska, Kansas

South, N = 76

Delaware, Maryland, District of Columbia, Virginia, West Virginia, North Carolina, South Carolina, Georgia, Florida, Kentucky, Tennessee, Alabama, Mississippi, Arkansas, Louisiana, Oklahoma, Texas

West, N = 60

Montana, Idaho, Wyoming, Colorado, New Mexico, Arizona, Utah, Nevada, Washington, Oregon, California, Alaska, Hawaii

Again, the first test is to see whether it is necessary to include separate regional coefficients in the two catgeories of distance. The F-test (comparing Equations 12 and 13 in Appendix B) yields a value of .35. Since $F_{.05}$ (n_1 = 3, n_2 = 301) $\doteq$ 2.65, the hypothesis of interaction can be rejected and the coefficients may be examined for the combined categories. These coefficients, for models excluding and including distance (Equations 14 and 13 in Appendix B) are shown in Table 4.5.

The coefficients in column 1 show that the only difference in frequency of contact is between the West and all other regions. Westerners maintain much less frequent contact with their parents than do inhabitants of other regions.

TABLE 4.5

Region Coefficients (Using MCA Convention) for Region Models of Parental
Contact, Excluding and Including Distance

Region	Excluding Distance	Including Distance
Northeast	.084	-.191
North Central	.136	.093
South	.230	-.016
West	-.626	.087

Mean Ln Contact = 2.790

But, of course, Westerners are more likely to have migrated and naturally their parents are likely to live further away than parents do in other regions; and this greater distance, in turn, explains their slighter propensity to visit. All regional differences are eliminated when distance is included. The F-test comparing the model whose coefficients are shown in column 2 of Table 4.5 to a simple distance model yields an F value of .84, whereas $F_{.05}$ ($n_1 = 3$, $n_2 = 304$) $\doteq$ 2.65. Thus, regional variation in parental contact does not require the introduction of any further explanatory variables, since there is no regional variation in contact remaining, once variation in distance is assumed.

Part III. Husband's Age and Father's Age

Hypotheses regarding the effect of age on parental contact are often, although not always, based on variation in distance between the residences of parent and child. One such hypothesis postulates a continuous decline in contact with the passage of time and therefore with the ages of both adult child and parent, and this is assumed to stem from the fact that "as the years go on, kin tend to live farther apart geographically," as Reiss (1962:336) remarks. The theory of a gradual drifting away from the family of orientation in response to the demands of occupation, health, or other factors is consistent with Parsons' (1943) conception of the progressive emancipation of the nuclear family from the family of orientation.

The second hypothesis, also based on distance, is that contact with parents is nonmonotonic with age — declining up to a point, then increasing again as the child and his parent grow older. The underlying assumption is that families live dispersed until such time as the needs of an aging parent require, or the retirement of either parent or child, or the greater control over the conditions of either's occupation allows the narrowing of the geographical distance between the two generations. Litwak, for example (1960), argues that the extended family coalesces when such coalescence is least likely to disrupt career paths or lead to financial strain. Thus he assumes that moves which bring the parents and adult children closer together are likely to involve retired people or job exchanges between people on the same occupational level.[9]

Aside from hypotheses based on distance (which imply that effects of age should disappear when distance is controlled), there are also hypotheses that, even if distance is held constant, age affects contact. Older people, lacking the contacts that younger people enjoy through work and participation in formal organizations, are likely to be more dependent on their adult children for companionship.[10] Furthermore, as Firth, Hubert and Forge (1969:105) point out, adult children are likely to feel an obligation to keep in touch with elderly parents more frequently than they would if the parents were younger and more self-sufficient.

These hypotheses bring up a question which has not been fully discussed in the literature: has age of adult son or age of parent the stronger effect upon the contact between them? Obviously, these variables are correlated; older parents are likely to have older children. Cross-sectionally, however, the two are not perfectly correlated, since people of different ages have children. Therefore, it is of interest to find out whether it is the age of parents or the age of children, if either or both, which affects parental contact. If contact depends on the needs or availability of the parent, then parent's age should be the more important, since the needs of parents and the freedom from conflicting demands on their time should both increase with age. On the other hand, the son's time is probably more valuable, so contacts are likely to be at his convenience; and his ease of movement and control of resources are usually greater, considerations which would make his age the more important. Control over resources, conflicting demands on time, and other factors need not have the same effect on contact; they merely indicate that the conditions and constraints of the child's situation are more important in determining contact than are those of the parent's.

Some of these hyptheses might better be considered in terms of changes in the family life cycle than of age. As Lansing and Kish (1957) demonstrate, changes in the life cycle explain more variance and are substantively more meaningful than changes in age. However, I do not have data on the life cycle and must therefore make do with the data available. The same tendencies which would be revealed by changes in the life cycle should also show up, although perhaps not as strongly, with age changes in the form of dummy variables. They do so in Lansing and Kish's study, and Aiken's data show the same trend of declining contact with husband's primary relatives, whether age or states in the life cycle are used.[11] Therefore I feel justified in using dummy variables to represent effects of age or life cycle, especially since the hypotheses to be tested are substantively meaningful in terms of changes in age.

Procedures and Findings

The dummy variables involved in this analysis include:

Age of Husband
15 - 24, N = 43
25 - 34, N = 132
35 - 44, N = 96
45 - 64, N = 39 (For ages 45-54, N = 30; for ages 55-64, N = 9).

Age of Husband's Father
   35 - 54, N = 74 (For ages 35-44, N = 11; for ages 45-54, N = 63).
   55 - 64, N = 106
   65 - 74, N = 79
   75 and over, N = 51 (For ages 75-84, N = 40; for ages 85-94,
             N = 10; for ages 95-104, N = 1).

Some categories cover more than ten years because the small frequencies in them necessitated combining them. Dummy variables were used in order to detect possible nonmonotonic effects which might be masked by the use of continuous variables.

Following my usual procedure, I began by analyzing the effects of age in the "same city" and "outside city" categories. In doing so, I compared models which included both husband's age, father's age, and distance (Equations 15 and 16 in Appendix B). The F-ratio obtained was 3.44, while $F_{.05}$ $(n_1 = 6, n_2 = 295) \doteq 2.14$. Therefore the hypothesis of interaction cannot be rejected—that is, the hypothesis of separate effects of age in the two distance categories, which now must be treated separately in the examination of the coefficients for husband's age and father's age (Table 4.6).

TABLE 4.6

Age Coefficients (Using MCA Convention) for Husband's and Father's Age Models, Excluding and Including Distance. Separate Age Effects for "Same City" and "Outside City" Categories

	Coefficients for Husbands in Same City as Father		Coefficients for Husbands Outside City of Father	
	Excluding Distance	Including Distance	Excluding Distance	Including Distance
Husband's Age				
15 - 24	.533	.533	-.289	-.025
25 - 34	-.102	-.102	.339	.133
35 - 44	-1.185	-1.185	.001	.153
45 - 64	.187	.187	-.139	-.119
Father's Age				
35 - 54	-.310	-.310	.291	.243
55 - 64	.171	.171	-.168	-.195
65 - 74	.169	.169	.073	-.102
75 and over	.002	.002	-.018	.056

Mean Ln Contact = 2.790

The coefficients for husband's age show large differences among husbands in the same city, whereas those for husbands elsewhere are much smaller, even before the continuous effect of distance is included (column 2). When distance is included these differences become negligible, indicating that age effects, if significant, are upon husbands who live in the same city as parents only. There are significant age effects, however, as demonstrated by an F-ratio of 2.94 obtained from a comparison of the complete age model shown in columns 3 and 4 of Table 4.6 (Equation 15 in Appendix B) to a model including distance only. $F_{.05}$ (n_1 = 12, n_2 = 295) $\doteq$ 1.80.

What is the relative importance of husband's age and father's age in determining frequency of contact? The differences between coefficients for father's age (Table 4.6) are, on the whole, small by comparison with those for husband's age, which indicates that the constraints on the opportunities in the son's situation exert more influence on visiting than those in the father's. This conclusion is supported by an F-test comparing the model represented in columns 3 and 4 of Table 4.6 (Equation 15 in Appendix B) to a model which includes the same terms except father's age (Equation 17 in Appendix B). The comparison makes it clear that, once husband's age is in the model, the increment to the variance explained by father's age variables is not significant: the F-ratio was .88, while $F_{.05}$ (n_1 = 6, n_2 = 2.95) $\doteq$ 2.14. It is not known what circumstances in the life situation of husbands control contact with parents—only that it is determined by characteristics related to ages of sons rather than of fathers.[12] How husband's age actually affects contact with his father is yet to be discovered, but it is known that age effects apparently occur only in the "same city" category. If the effects in the same city contribute all of the variance explained by age differences, a simpler model will do which allows only these effects, plus distance (Equation 18 in Appendix B). Father's age as a source of variation in contact already has been eliminated, and an F-test comparing models including and excluding the age coefficients for husbands outside the city (Equations 17 and 18) shows that the latter do not contribute significantly to the explained variance: F = .24; $F_{.05}$ (n_1 =3, n_2 = 301) $\doteq$ 2.65. Thus the F-tests support the impression that the only differences worth interpreting are those between the coefficients for husband's age of those living in the same city as their fathers. The coefficients for this simpler model (Table 4.7) show that the relationship between parental contact and husband's age is nonmonotonic in husbands in father's city, being lowest in those in their middle years—presumably the period when the demands on their time are greatest and leisure time is spent either with the family of procreation or with business friends and others who are not relatives. That contact increases in the period between 45 and 64 may reflect the needs of parents who have reached retirement; the husband's own children are now likely to demand little time, since they will probably have left home.

The possibility cannot be ruled out that the observed differences in contact of husbands in the same city as parents actually arise in differences in distance within the city. In fact, it is easy to theorize that the differences observed might be due to the greater proportion of husbands at the lower end of the age continuum (ages 15 to 24) who still live in the household of the family of orientation, and the greater proportion of husbands at the upper end of the

TABLE 4.7

Age Coefficients (Using MCA Convention) for Husband's Age Model
with Distance, Allowing Varying Age Coefficients for Husbands
in the "Same City" Category Only

Husband's Age	Coefficients for Husbands in Same City as Father	Coefficients for Husbands Outside City of Father
15 - 24	.270	.208
25 - 34	-.085	.208
35 - 44	-1.116	.208
45 - 64	.208	.208

Mean Ln Contact = 2.790

age continuum (ages 45 to 64) who share their own household with their
elderly parents.

A crude test of this hypothesis is made by adjusting the expected values of
contact in each age group to the probability, differing with age, that parents
live in the son's household. Based on data from the 1960 Census, estimates of
the proportion of husband-wife households which include parents of the head
of household among heads classified in three age groups are: .0299 where
heads are under 35, .0553 where heads are aged 35-64, and .0136 where
heads are 65+.[13] If it is assumed that these proportions apply to the husbands in the present sample, these figures can be used to estimate how many
husbands in each category may be expected to have their parents living with
them.

For example, in my total sample of husbands whose age is reported (N =
1061), there are 76 aged 15-24. Of these 76, I assume that .0299 have parents
of either husband or wife living with them. Since they are unlikely to live with
both sets of parents, I assume that, at most, .0150 of the 76 live with husband's father. This means that approximately 1.14 husbands, aged 15-24 live
with their fathers. Rounding this value to 1, it is, of course, assumed that
this one husband is in the subsample of husbands whose fathers are living and
are in the same city. There are 28 husbands aged 15-24 in the same city. Assuming that the one who lives with his father sees him every day, he is assigned a value of ln contact = 5.899 (= ln 365) and the expected value is
computed for the other 27 husbands that would be necessary to obtain the
expected value actually obtained from regression. The actual expected ln
contact values, number in the total sample, number in the "same city" category, assumed proportion living with husband's father, expected number
living with husband's father, and adjusted expected ln contact values, are
presented in Table 4.8.

If the adjusted values shown in column 7 of Table 4.8 are expressed as increments over the value expected for those aged 45-64, increments are obtained of

TABLE 4.8

Adjusted Expected Values of Ln Contact, Assuming Varying Proportions of Husbands by Age in the Same City Whose Parents are Alive and Live in the Same Household

Husband's Age	Expected Ln Contact from Table 4.7	Number in Total Sample	Number in Same City as Father	Assumed Proportion Living with Husband's Father	Assumed Number Living with Husband's Father	Adjusted Expected ln Contact
15-24	4.712	76	28	.0150	1	4.668
25-34	4.357	268	54	.0150	4	4.234
35-44	3.326	301	38	.0276	8	2.640
45-64	4.650	416	17	.0276	11	2.359

2.308 for husbands aged 15-24, 1.875 for those aged 25-34, 0.280 for those aged 35-44, and 0.000 for those aged 45-64. Thus the pattern of differences by age is strongly affected by the varying probabilities of having living parents and of sharing a household with them.

This is particularly true of the coefficient for husbands aged 45-64. If the greater probability is taken into account that these husband's fathers died or that the fathers live in the same household with them, then, were it not for these tendencies, this group would have the lowest rate of contact. The coefficients for age of husbands in the same city as parents would then show a tendency to decrease monotonically with increasing age of husbands. In other words, a husband between the ages of 45 and 64 whose father is alive and living in the same city is very likely to have his father living with him; but if not, then he is less likely to see his father than he would be at a younger age.

These adjusted coefficients should not be given too much weight since they were based on crude estimates and several assumptions, yet the tendency for contact to decrease with age, once the increasing probability of living with parents is taken into account, may be due to differences in distance within the city. That is, as sons grow older they may live further away from parents. even though in the same city. However, the fact that there was no such monotonic pattern among respondents living outside the city of parents, before distance was controlled, suggests that differences in distance by age cannot explain the presumed decrease in parental contact by age in respondents living in the same city as their parents but not in the same household. Other circumstances, such as increasing occupational and familial demands on the time of husbands up to the age of retirement (the husbands with living fathers in my sample are all under 65 years old and all but nine are under 55), or the greater likelihood, with increasing age, of having incapacitated parents who cannot reciprocate their children's visits may account for the decreasing adjusted frequencies in contact, if these actually reflect reality.

The fact that the patterns of parental contact by age of husbands differ as between respondents in the same city and those outside it follows from the impossibility of living with parents, if the latter do not reside in the same city. More generally, however, the absence of age effects outside the city suggest that living outside the city of an elderly father's residence makes one unavailable for the expected familial responsibilities. One can neither keep up a daily watch by living with him, nor provide constant companionship by living near him. It is possible then that these responsibilities devolve upon a sibling or other relative who is physically closer or who actually lives with the parent, leaving the contacts of the respondent who lives outside the city unsusceptible to age changes.

Such speculation is obviously tentative but it fits the descriptions found in case studies of elderly people as being in most cases far from isolated. They are as a rule in close contact with at least one son or daughter who lives close by and the members of the family act as functional equivalents or substitutes for one another in serving their needs. As Townsend, for example, puts it (1955:190):

What is evident is that for most older people the lack of a spouse or of children is not often a crippling handicap, for the simple reason that they usually have other relatives who act as replacements or substitutes within the circle of intimate kin of three or four generations.

Summary

The age of husbands has a significant and nonmonotonic effect on contact with parents, whereas the age of parents does not affect contact once the age of husbands is allowed to do so. This may reflect the greater importance of the situation of the husband: his time is more valuable and he has greater control over the resources with which to initiate contact. Nevertheless, he may initiate contact in response to the needs of an aging parent. Age affects parental contact only among husbands who live in the same city as parents. Both the youngest and the oldest husbands are in more frequent contact with their fathers than those in the two middle age groups. By taking into account the probability of having living parents and the greater probability, as age increases (up to the age of 64, at least), that they and their fathers live in the same household, the greater frequency of contact of husbands aged 45 to 64 can easily be attributed to the circumstance that a higher proportion of those with living fathers share households with them. When this tendency is accounted for, husbands in the same city as their fathers show, with age, a monotonic decline in frequency of contact. Finally, it may be that the absence of age effects in husbands outside the city reflects the obvious fact that they cannot provide companionship or constant service to aging parents requiring almost daily attention. In this case, responsibility may be assumed by siblings or other relatives closer at hand.

Part IV. A Summary Model

Do the variables found to affect parental contact directly (i.e., even when distance is included in the model) still affect contact in a model which includes all such variables?

It is possible that the variance explained by one factor (one set of dummy variables) overlaps or is the same as the variance explained by another; in other words, the two factors are not independent and the same explained variance is simply being attributed to two different explanatory variables. But this seems unlikely, since the only variables found to have significant effects besides those conveyed through distance are ehtnicity in the case of the sample as a whole and age of husband in the case of husbands in the same city. It is unlikely that these variables are sufficiently correlated to overlap much in explaining variance; however, for the sake of completeness, I present them, together with distance, as the final model of parental contact on the basis of the investigation up to this point. The model (Equation 19 in Appendix B), includes a single set of ethnicity coefficients for the combined sample, a set of age coefficients for husbands in the same city as their fathers, an "outside city" coefficient, and a coefficient for the continuous effect of ln distance.

The ethnicity coefficients in Table 4.9 when compared with those in column 2 of Table 4.1, are seen to be hardly changed by the inclusion of age. The order of the Irish and Scandinavians is reversed, but the two were so similar before that the difference between them was and is negligible. The remaining coefficients retain their order and their approximate magnitude, as do also

TABLE 4.9

All MCA Coefficients for Parental Contact Model Including Ethnicity,
Age, and Distance

	Coefficients for Husbands in Same City as Father	Coefficients for Husbands Outside City of Father
Ethnicity		
Irish	.444	.444
Scandinavian	.513	.513
Eastern European	.169	.169
French, Spanish, Italian	.018	.018
English, Scottish, U.S.A. White	-.042	-.042
German, Dutch, Swiss	-.206	-.206
Nonwhite and Other	-.265	-.265
Age of Husband		
15-24	.288	.205
25-34	-.106	.205
35-44	-1.085	.205
45-64	.205	.205

Distance Coefficients

-.300 - .683 (0 - 2.853)   .238 - .683 (1n D_i - 2.853)

Mean Ln Contact = 2.790

R^2 = .6794

the age coefficients, which can be compared to those in Table 4.7. Here again there is no meaningful change in the sets of coefficients, so that the effect of age can be considered as independent of ethnicity. Both these observations are confirmed by F-tests which show that the effect of ethnicity remains significant when age is included in the model   (F = 2.21; $F_{.05}$ (n_1 = 6, n_2 = 298) $\doteq$ 214);   and the effect of age remains significant when ethnicity is included in the model   (F = 9.49; $F_{.05}$ (n_1 = 3, n_2 = 298) $\doteq$ 2.65).   However, the effect of age is considerably stronger than that of ethnicity: age contributes an additional 3.11 percent to the variance explained by a model which already includes ethnicity and distance, whereas ethnicity contributes only 1.45 percent to a model including age and distance. The conclusion, then, is that, aside from distance, age and ethnicity are the only two additional variables which directly influence parental contact; and age does so only in the case of husbands who live in the same city as their fathers.

FOOTNOTES

[1] This strategy entails the risk that the effects of variables may be suppressed by correlated variables and come to light only when those other variables are included in the model. In the present case the possibilities of this occurring seemed slight, since the variables involved should not be highly correlated with one another. I therefore decided that, rather than devote a considerable proportion of the analysis to the possible existence of suppressed effects, it would be more fruitful to concentrate on detailed study of those effects which the analysis shows to exist and about which meaningful substantive questions can be raised and perhaps answered.

[2] See Locke (1940); Bossard and Boll (1946). Gans (1962:46) also discusses but does not offer reasons for the limited ties between the immigrant generation in Italian families and the generation which follows it. Garigue and Firth (1956) and Campisi (1948), stress the continued existence of close family ties between first- and second-generation Italians, but Campisi also points out the weakened bond between the generations.

[3] A discussion of the causes of family disorganization or of the "culture of poverty" would be out of place here, so I shall not attempt it. For recent elaboration and study of some of the questions involved, see the articles in Moynihan (1969).

[4] At least one writer describes a particular settlement of Norwegians as characterized by strong family cohesion: Munch (1949).

[5] Laumann (1969:183) summarizes some of the literature bearing on this argument. None of it applies directly to religious differences in family structure or cohesion, but the existence of religious differences in other social phenomena might suggest that there are religious differences in family contact, as well. Such differences, however, may be caused by the differential distribution of some other variable by religion, rather than by religion itself. For example, both Gockel (1969) and Goldstein (1969) find that observed religious differentials in income are attributable to the educational composition of religious groups. One could, however, regard the religious differences as causally prior to the educational and income differences.

[6] There is one exception. In the amount of total contact with all of husband's and wife's relatives in the Detroit area combined (Table 44, p. 145), he finds that Jews maintain the most contact, with Catholics second, and Protestants third. This measure (total contact) is affected by the differential availability of relatives. Robins and Tomanec (1962) find, using a combined measure of "family closeness" that Jews are "closer" to relatives than Protestants and Catholics. The confirmation of this finding by Winch, Greer, and Blumberg (1967:267) has already been discussed.

[7] The multidimensionality of the urban-rural continuum has been pointed out by Duncan (1957).

[8] Others who have speculated on regional differences in the family include Vance (1948), Folsom (1948), Cavan (1948), and Hayner (1948).

[9] Willmott and Young (1960:38-39) declare but do not demonstrate that older people live closer to their adult children. Cavan (1949) cites data from the 1940 Census which show that the percentage of males, aged 60 and over, who live with children or other relatives increases with age. The same is true of females. Rosenmayr (1968), reviewing various studies, finds support for the hypothesis that the elderly live close to and maintain ties with their adult children. Burgess (1960) also summarizes studies in several countries on the relationships between adult children and their parents.

[10] Wilensky (1961) cites several studies which find that participation in formal organizations drops off, following a peak period in the 40's. Loomis (1936:188) also notes in regard to North Carolina farm families, that activity outside the home is greatest before children arrive: "With the addition of children this activity away from home decreases, both because the children are a burden, and because they make family home life more intensive. When the parents are old, they are either too infirm to take up outside activity again, or they satisfy themselves with contacts with their children's families."

[11] See his data (1964) for "husband's primary" relatives in Table 52 (p. 165) and 55 (p. 169). Aiken's data do not separate sibling contacts from parental contacts, so it is questionable whether his findings on age are comparable to those in the present study of parental contacts only.

[12] This finding is similar to those in the preceding chapter—that the coefficients for father's occupation are very similar to one another, and that farm background, a characteristic of fathers, rather than of sons, does not affect contact.

[13] These figures are derived from data on husband-wife families in the United States Census of Population: 1960, PC(2)-4A, Table 18, p. 170.

CHAPTER 5

THE INTERDEPENDENCE OF
CONTACTS WITH RELATIVES

Introduction

Students of kinship ties have often declared that they are interdependent. Among them are Firth, Hubert, and Forge (1969:450), who write:

Behavior towards people recognized as "relatives" is not random; it tends to follow prescribed conventions, to be repetitive and to form part of articulated series of relationships in which ties with any one kinsman are affected by those with other kin.

Bott (1957:143) speaks of "connecting relatives . . . who control and direct the flow of activities and social relationships." Young and Willmott (1957:58) claim that the mother is the main link between siblings, since sons and daughters are likely to meet at her home. Mogey (1956:78) makes the same point. According to Townsend (1955:190) and Willmott and Young (1960:57), members of the family play interchangeable roles; in fact, a function of the extended family is to provide substitutes for missing members. Irish (1964:282) states that siblings may act as substitutes for parents, but only when certain members of the family are missing — which does not mean direct interdependence of contacts. The point that members of the family can replace one another is fulfilling kinship obligations is corroborated, for example, by Firth (1964:82); and Firth and Djamour (1956:59). Their theory of substitutability contradicts the hypothesis of the connecting link under certain circumstances, since the latter implies that visits with certain kin reduce the likelihood of visits with the others, whereas the former makes the point that visits with certain kin (e.g., parents) increase the likelihood of visits with other kin (e.g., siblings). It is possible, however, that both phenomena operate in specific situations or in regard to specific relatives.

Another formulation of the theory of interdependence is that kin, especially the more distantly related, are most likely to meet on ritual or ceremonial occasions (see, e.g., Loudon, 1961:346). Here the relationships among contacts are based on their mutual dependence on a third factor—ceremonial occasions or family celebrations—to bring relatives together. Moreover, visits with the more distantly related may be incidental to visits with the more closely related, as Adams (1968:145 ff.) points out.

Despite the numerous and varied formulations of the interdependence of relatives, there is almost no quantitative evidence of it. Aiken (1964:87-92) is the only one who, as far as I know, has tried to test the hypothesis that having a living mother increase one's contact with other relatives: he finds that if wife's mother is alive, visits to both husband's and wife's primary relatives (each grouped separately) in the Detroit area are increased.[1] In what follows I will test some specific hypotheses about the interdependence of contacts with various relatives and suggest the direction which further research might take. The results should not be regarded as other than exploratory for the number of cases is often very small, and different samples are used for different problems. Furthermore, the data are limited so that in testing hypotheses I have had to make use of father as a crucial or connecting relative, although most writers indicate that mother actually exerts more significant effects.

Existence and Location of Father

The first hypotheses to be considered are those that begin with the question: does knowing anything about where or whether father lives tell anything about frequency of the son's contact with other relatives? It is easy to think of reasons why knowing whether father lives might improve the prediction of contact with other relatives. Will, for example, contact with a brother be more frequent if the father is alive than if he is dead? When father is alive there are more ceremonial occasions to draw the family together (e.g. father's birthday or wedding anniversary, assuming mother, too, is alive). Furthermore, father's house may provide a meeting place for siblings, as Mogey (1956:78) and Young and Willmott (1957:58) found in the case of mother.

In my data there are seven possible combinations of existence and location of father and oldest brother:
1. father and oldest brother live in same city as respondent.
2. father and oldest brother live in same city; neither lives in respondent's city.[2]
3. father and oldest brother live in different cities; neither lives in respondent's city.
4. father lives in respondent's city; oldest brother lives in a different city.
5. oldest brother lives in respondent's city; father lives in a different city.
6. father dead; oldest brother lives in respondent's city.
7. father dead; oldest brother lives in a different city.

(For the N's of each of these relatives, see Appendix D.) The categories do not take into account respondent's distance from father or brother, or the distance between the two, but distance is conceptualized as a continuous variable which will be controlled by inclusion in the model when comparisons are made.

One would expect the lowest rates of contact with brother in categories 6

THE INTERDEPENDENCE OF CONTACTS WITH RELATIVES

and 7, in both of which father is dead. One might expect similar rates of contact in categories 2 and 4, since contact does not necessarily depend on initiation by the respondent and in both, father and a brother live in the same city, the brother being the respondent in category 4. When father and brother live in the same city, which is different from respondent's city, contact may be initiated more frequently by respondent, because he can visit both father and brother simultaneously. If, on the other hand, respondent and father live in the same city, with brother elsewhere, brother may make trips more frequently to visit both relatives simultaneously.

There are many other possible combinations of kinsman and father's residence, not all of which will be independent. For example, one could compare categories 1 and 5, in both of which brother lives in respondent's city. In category 1, however, where father also lives in respondent's city, one might expect that contact with brother would be more frequent—if, as I assume, contact with siblings is mediated by parents and likely to occur on ritual occasions involving parents. Alternatively, if the siblings provide one another with direct assistance and/or companionship, then contact with each other may not depend on the presence of father. Another possibility covered by category 1 is that the presence of all three relatives in the same city is in itself an indication of a familial orientation, reflected, for example, in a high rate of visiting brother; but this would not be instigated directly by the presence of father in the same city. None of these hypotheses, however, is supported by my data although, to repeat, the findings should be regarded as tentative.

I will now discuss in detail the effect of existence and location of father on contact with oldest brother. Since the findings concerning other relatives are very similar, most of them will be summarized briefly. The method is the dummy variable regression analysis already described and, again, the conventions of multiple classification analysis are followed in presenting the findings. Each person receives a score consisting of the grand mean plus a coefficient specific to the category of which he is a member. There are seven coefficients, corresponding to the seven categories listed above.

The MCA coefficients for ln contact with oldest brother are presented in Table 5.1, in models which exclude and include ln distance from him. When ln distance from brother is excluded, large differences appear in the coefficients. However, all the categories with large positive increments are those in which brother is in the same city as respondent, suggesting that distance from brother is the cause of the differences. In fact, once distance is included in the model, the large positive increments become small and negative. It might seem strange that the mean of ln contact with brother is reduced if brother lives in the same city. This result is actually an artifact of the discontinuity in the data between the "same city" category and distances outside the city which makes it difficult to detect any other patterns of the coefficients. However, an F-test comparing the model to one including only distance and coefficients for brothers inside and outside respondent's city (models 2 and 3 in Appendix C) reveals that in any case there are no significant effects other than those of distance: $F = .429$; $F_{.05}$ $(n_1 = 5, n_2 = 339) \doteq 2.26$. Thus the null hypothesis cannot be rejected that knowing whether and where father lives has no effect upon the reliability of predictions of the frequency of contact with oldest brother.

TABLE 5.1

MCA Coefficients for Ln Contacts with Oldest Brother (OB) by Existence of and location of Father (F)

	MCA Coefficients	
Categories of Existence and Location	Excluding Distance	Including Distance
1. F and OB in Respondent's City	1.843	-.166
2. F and OB in Same City; Neither in Respondent's City	- .691	.249
3. F and OB in Different Cities; Neither in Respondent's City	-1.084	.338
4. F in Respondent's City; OB in Different City	- .813	.464
5. OB in Respondent's City; F in Different City	1.614	-.395
6. F Dead; OB in Respondent's City	1.603	-.406
7. F Dead; OB in Different City	-1.258	.153
Mean Ln Contacts = 2.145		

The same general conclusion is obtained for ln contacts with husband of oldest married sister (HOMS), male cousin (MC), father's oldest brother (FOB), and mother's oldest brother (MOB).[4] In each case large differences which appear in the coefficients when distance from the relative is not included in the model disappear when distance is included, and F-tests show that knowledge about the existence and location of one's father (in the form of the model presented as Equation 2 in Appendix C) does not improve prediction of contact with any of the other relatives.

Would a simpler model which allows only parameters for a living in contrast to a dead father together with distance parameters show a significant effect of father's existence — even though the more complex model presented above attributes no significant effects to father's existence and location? In order to show how small such effects are, Table 5.2 presents the differences between coefficients for a living as opposed to a dead father and the percentage increment added to a simple distance model by the inclusion of these parameters (Equations 4 and 3 in Appendix C).

In each case, the difference is positive, which means that respondents with living fathers visit each of the other relatives slightly more frequently, but the increment in explained variance is less than .6 percent. None of these differences is significant as determined by F-tests comparing the model including the parameters for a living as contrasted with a dead father to that including distance alone (models 4 and 3 in Appendix C). Neither the existence nor the location of father is shown on the basis of the present data to affect contact with other relatives.

TABLE 5.2

Differences Between Coefficients for Living vs. Dead Father and
Increment Added to Variance Explained by Ln Distance Models
for Ln Contacts with Five Relatives

Ln Contacts with:	Differences Between Coefficients for Living vs. Dead Father	Percent Increment Added to Explained Variance
OB	.196	.21
HOMS	.134	.12
MC	.228	.43
FOB	.012	.00
MOB	.209	.52

Contact with Father

Even though father's existence and location apparently do not affect contact with other relatives, it is possible that the frequency of contact with father may affect its frequency with other relatives. If, for example, visits to genealogically more distant relatives are contingent on or incidental to visits to kin more closely connected (as Adams, 1968:145 ff. argues), then visiting father might have a positive effect on visiting the others. Moreover, father's house may encourage contact with other relatives by providing a common meeting ground.

The effect of contact with father on contact with other relatives may also be dependent on a third variable, which has not been measured; namely, the distance between father and the other relative. This may act as a covariate, in that, as the distance between father and, let us say, brother increases, visits to father become less and less likely to affect visits to brother. If father lives 100 miles away from respondent, and brother lives five miles away from father, then when visiting father respondent is likely to see brother as well, perhaps because the additional cost is small, or because the three can meet at a common meeting place. If, however, father lives 100 miles away and brother lives 100 miles away from father, then a visit to father is less likely to inspire respondent to combine with it a visit to brother, if there is no occasion for bringing all three together; in fact, the expenditure of time and money on the visit to father may preclude a visit to brother. Since I do not know the distance between the two relatives, I cannot include it as a continuous covariate. Therefore, the slopes must be considered as averages over the various distances between relatives.

If distance from father may be expected to affect visits to other relatives, one possibility is that the farther one travels to visit father, the surer one will be to include other relatives in the visit. For one thing, the farther one lives from father, the more likely one is to visit only on ceremonial occasions, and so the greater the likelihood of seeing other relatives. The relationship could also be more direct, in that the greater the distance or cost of visiting father, the more likely one is to plan the trip so that other relatives can be seen along the way. Still another possibility is that the farther one lives from father, the more likely one is to substitute for visits to him visits to other relatives, to preserve the family ties or to satisfy familial obligations.

In testing the general hypothesis connecting visits to remoter kin with distance and visits to father, I have, naturally, used only those respondents whose father and other relative in question were alive.[5] Preliminary models of contact with each relative included five categories of location of father and other relative, corresponding to the first five categories in the preceding section. The complete model of, say, ln contact with oldest brother (Equation 6 in Appendix C) includes separate intercepts for each category; separate slopes for ln distance from brother in categories 2, 3, and 4 (where brother is outside respondent's city); separate slopes for ln distance from father in categories 3 and 5 (where father is outside respondent's city); and separate slopes for ln contacts with father in each of the five categories.[6] However, F-tests of the models for each relative indicated that it is unnecessary to allow separate intercepts or separate slopes for any of the variables. The model therefore has been simplified, with separate intercepts for relatives inside and outside respondent's city, a single slope for ln distance from relative, a single slope for ln distance from father, and a single slope for ln contacts with father.[7] The parameter estimates for this model of ln contacts with each of the five available relatives are shown in Table 5.3.

TABLE 5.3

Regression Parameter Estimates of ln Contact Regression Models
for Five Relatives; Models Include Separate Intercepts for
Relatives Inside and Outside Respondent's City, Distance
From Relative, Distance from Father, and Ln Contacts with Father

Ln Contact With:	Intercept for Relative Inside R's City	Intercept for Relative Outside R's City	Slope of Ln D from Relative	Slope of Ln D from Father	Slope of Ln C with Father	N
OB	1.605	2.079	-.572	.279	.463	125
HOMS	1.781	2.070	-.577	.285	.373	120
MC	1.593	1.336	-.381	.195	.276	188
FOB	1.530	.226	-.202	.202	.272	92
MOB	2.811	2.471	-.350	.021	.015	121

According to the models present in Table 5.3, distance from each relative has a negative effect on contact with him. (All these slopes can be interpreted as elasticities — the percentage change in contact for a percentage change in distance from relative, distance from father, or contact with father. (See Chapter 2.) Both ln distance and ln contact with father have positive effects on ln contact with each relative, and on every relative except MOB these effects are significant, as indicated by F-tests comparing a model with each of these parameters to one including only parameters for distance from the relative in question (Equations 7 and 8 compared with Equation 3 in Appendix C). It is interesting to note that all of the slopes for the OB and HOMS model are larger in absolute value than those for the genealogically more distant relative. This suggests that visits to less closely related relatives are less vulnerable to changes in other variables, including distance from and contact with father, as well as distance from the relatives themselves. If these models are accepted as adequate representations of the interdependence of contacts between pairs of relatives, then the conclusion is that contact with father has a direct positive effect on contacts with other relatives, and that distance from father also has a direct positive effect on contacts with other relatives, for any of the reasons discussed above.

This model might be regarded as unsatisfactory in several respects. For one thing, it assumes that the interdependence of contacts is unidirectional; that is, that contact with father affects contact with brother, whereas the reverse is not the case. Such an assumption is unwarranted *a priori*, since the same arguments that have been made about the effect of distance from and contact with father on contact with brother, for example, can also be made in reverse for the effect of distance from and contact with brother on contact with father. Furthermore, in the regression models it is assumed that the entire relationship between contact with father and contact with another relative is represented by the direct effect of the former on the latter, plus the common causes present in the model—namely the distances separating the two. That is, the model assumes that there are no common causes of these contact variables other than those appearing in the model. This assumption can perhaps be seen more clearly in Figure 5.1, a path diagram of the model.[8]

The parameters estimated in this model are simply the regression coefficients for the regression of X_3 on X_2 and X_1 and the regression of X_4 on X_3, X_2 and X_1. In Table 5.3 the unstandardized forms of the coefficients b, c, and e were presented. The coefficients a and d were not estimated. Figure 5.1 makes clear a basic property of least squares linear regression; namely, that the residuals of variables determined in the model are uncorrelated with the residuals of their predictor variables. In other words, the two contact variables are assumed to have no common causes other than those included in the model. This assumption is unwarranted since many obvious common causes have not been included in the model. One can posit, for example, among certain individuals a familial orientation or feeling of obligation which motivates them to visit all their relatives more frequently than others do. The frequency of ceremonial occasions or family re-unions might also be conceptualized as a variable which though not included in the model, could affect contacts with each relative, aside from their direct effects on each other. These are only two plausible sources of a possible residual correlation between the two contact variables—enough to show why the previous model may be considered inadequate.

FIGURE 5.1

Path Diagram of Regression Model for Determination of Contacts
with Two Relatives

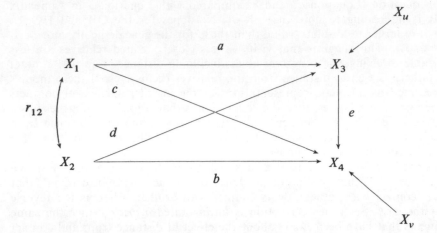

X_1 – 1n distance from relative A X_u – unidentified (residual) causes of X_3
X_2 – 1n distance from relative B X_v – unidentified (residual) causes of X_4
X_3 – 1n contacts with relative A
X_4 – 1n contacts with relative B

The Model   Assumptions

$$X_{3i} = aX_{1i} + dX_{2i} + uX_{ui}$$ $$r_{1u} = r_{2u} = r_{1v} = r_{2v} = r_{3v} = r_{uv} = 0$$
$$X_{4i} = bX_{2i} + cX_{1i} + eX_{3i} + vX_{vi}$$

An Alternative Model

An alternative model which does not suffer from the inadequacies of the
regression model discussed above is presented in Figure 5.2. In this model,
contact with father is assumed to have a direct effect on contact with brother,
for example, and vice versa. However, there are assumed to be no direct effects of distance from brother on contact with father. If such effects were included, the model would be underidentified and further assumptions or constraints would be required to obtain a solution.[9]

This model can be thought of as representing the demand for each of two
relatives (as measured by the frequency of contact with each of them), where
demand for relative A is a function of both the cost (distance) of visiting him
and the demand for relative B. The demand for relative B is a function of the
cost (distance) of a visit to him and the demand for relative A but cost affects
only the demand for relative A indirectly by affecting the demand for relative
B, which directly affects the demand for relative A. This conceptualization in

FIGURE 5.2

Path Diagram of a Model for Simultaneous Determination
of Contacts with Two Relatives

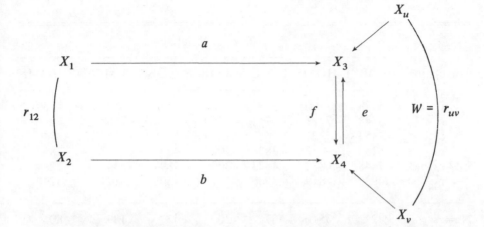

X_1 — ln distance from relative A $\qquad$ X_u — unidentified (residual) causes of X_3

X_2 — ln distance from relative B $\qquad$ X_v — unidentified (residual) causes of X_4

X_3 — ln contacts with relative A

X_4 — ln contacts with relative B

The Model $\hspace{4cm}$ Assumptions

$$X_{3i} = aX_{1i} + eX_{4i} + uX_{ui}$$

$$X_{4i} = bX_{2i} + fX_{3i} + vX_{vi}$$

$$r_{1u} = r_{2u} = r_{1v} = r_{2v} = 0$$

terms of demand functions is useful if one thinks of relatives in economic terms as being either complementary, in the sense that contact with one increases the likelihood of contact with another, or competitive, as various authors have argued, so that visits to one tend to preclude visits to another. The reasons for possible positive or negative effects have been mentioned earlier and need not be repeated here. However, another notable feature of this model is that, regardless of the direct effects of the dependent variables on one another, it also allows the residuals of the dependent variables to be correlated. Thus it permits estimation of the magnitude of other sources of common variance in the dependent variables besides those actually measured in the model, although it does not give any idea about what those sources might be.

The parameters for this model can not be estimated by least-squares linear regression; however, they are equivalent to those obtained by the technique known as indirect least-squares.[10] The correlations used in estimating the parameters for models involving several pairs of relatives are presented in Table 5.4.

TABLE 5.4

Correlations for Models with Simultaneous Dependence of Ln Contacts
with Each of Seven Pairs of Relatives (Model Shown in Figure 2).
Variable Subscripts Correspond to Those in Figure 5.2

			Pairs of Relatives				
Correlations	F-OB	F-HOMS	F-MC	F-FOB	F-MOB	OB-MC	OB-HOMS
r_{12}	.5978	.7590	.5153	.5362	.5157	.3509	.4739
r_{13}	-.8848	-.7771	-.8714	-.6740	-.8726	-.7468	-.7206
r_{14}	-.4454	-.5321	-.2963	-.1609	-.1478	-.2718	-.3848
r_{23}	-.5150	-.5052	-.3828	-.2077	-.4208	-.2427	-.2862
r_{24}	-.7348	-.6872	-.4573	-.3007	-.4899	-.5403	-.7294
r_{34}	.4930	.4819	.3500	.2717	.1508	.2121	.3290
N =	42	35	57	30	45	109	80

These correlations involve only respondents of whom both of the relatives in question live in different cities, neither of which is the respondent's home (category 3 in earlier models in this chapter). The reason for using only such respondents was that for them alone the distance from both relatives is a meaningful variable. It should be kept in mind that the very small N's make these models exceedingly tentative; and direct comparisons cannot be made to the previous models because of the differences in respondents involved. The present models are presented merely to suggest the form future models may take, given more cases and more of the relevant variables.

The equations with unstandardized coefficients for the model represented in Figure 5.2 are shown in Table 5.5. Together with the models of the contact of father and another relative, models of contact between two pairs of relatives aside from father are shown, to see whether they follow the same pattern as the pairs involving father. Also shown in Table 5.5 are the correlations of the residuals of each pair of contact variables.

In general, the coefficients for the models are quite reasonable, an exception being the model of F-FOB contacts, which are based on the smallest N. In the case of each pair of relatives, contact between them is negatively affected by their distance from each other. In all the models involving father, contact with the other relative has a negative direct effect on contact with father, while in three of the five models contact with father has a very small positive direct effect on contact with the other, but it is, in all cases, negligible — ranging from -.095 to +.059. However, in some cases the effect of contact with the other relative on contact with father is quite strong (for example, F-HOMS, F-MC, and F-FOB).

It is difficult to know whether to attach substantive significance to these

TABLE 5.5

Equations with Unstandardized Coefficients for Ln Contact with Pairs
of Relatives (Model Shown in Figure 5.2) and w ($= r_{uv}$)
for Each Model

Pairs of Relatives	Equation			W
F-OB	$\ln C^F$	$= 6.365 - .912 \ln D^F$	$- .032 \ln C^{OB}$	
	$\ln C^{OB}$	$= 5.348 - .763 \ln D^{OB}$	$+ .010 \ln C^F$	.376
F-HOMS	$\ln C^F$	$= 6.888 - 1.013 \ln D^F$	$- .442 \ln C^{HOMS}$	
	$\ln C^{HOMS}$	$= 3.202 - .431 \ln D^{HOMS}$	$+ .018 \ln C^F$	.531
F-MC	$\ln C^F$	$= 6.513 - .913 \ln D^F$	$- .330 \ln C^{MC}$	
	$\ln C^{MC}$	$= 2.302 - .322 \ln D^{MC}$	$+ .059 \ln C^F$	.535
F-FOB	$\ln C^F$	$= 6.378 - .786 \ln D^F$	$- 1.451 \ln C^{FOB}$	
	$\ln C^{FOB}$	$= 1.488 - .184 \ln D^{FOB}$	$- .000 \ln C^F$	.799
F-MOB	$\ln C^F$	$= 6.371 - .853 \ln D^F$	$- .119 \ln C^{MOB}$	
	$\ln C^{MOB}$	$= 3.131 - .404 \ln D^{MOB}$	$- .095 \ln C^F$	.298
OB-MC	$\ln C^{OB}$	$= 4.662 - .642 \ln D^{OB}$	$- .068 \ln C^{MC}$	
	$\ln C^{MC}$	$= 1.994 - .296 \ln D^{MC}$	$+ .079 \ln C^{OB}$	-.010
OB-HOMS	$\ln C^{OB}$	$= 4.388 - .599 \ln D^{OB}$	$- .090 \ln C^{HOMS}$	
	$\ln C^{HOMS}$	$= 3.946 - .539 \ln D^{HOMS}$	$+ .075 \ln C^{OB}$	.220

coefficients, given their possible instability and the smallness of the sample.
However, the general impression seems to be that in the matter of contact,
genealogically more distant kin compete with the more closely related, pre-

sumably because of the cost. Since the reverse is not generally true, this is not easy to explain. One possibility is that contact with more distantly related kin has stronger effects on contact with closer kin than vice versa, simply because more closely-related kin are more easily affected by all relevant variables, as is shown in the elasticity of their contacts with respect to distance. However, this pattern is not valid for all the relatives (i.e., the coefficient for $\ln C^{OB}$ is less than that for $\ln C^{HOMS}$, $\ln C^{MC}$, and $\ln C^{FOB}$ in their effects on $\ln C^{F}$).

A much more speculative and less general interpretation is that contacts with genealogically more distant kin reflect voluntary behavior, whereas contacts with parents are more likely to be considered obligatory even though also more responsive to change in distance; and people who visit voluntarily, that is, who maintain contacts without regard to the degree of genealogical relationship, are less likely to regard a visit as an obligation which must be frequently performed. The reverse would not be the case, since feelings of obligation to parents may also indicate similar but weaker ties of obligation to other kin; or they may simply reflect the selective obligation of which Firth, for example, has written (1964:82).

Interpretation of differences among the coefficients is extremely hazardous, and should not be taken too seriously. Nevertheless, the consistent negative effect of contact with genealogically more distant relatives on contact with closer relatives should be noted, since further analysis with better data and more of the relevant variables may clarify it or show it disappears.

A finding of perhaps greater importance is of sizeable positive residual correlations between the two contact variables, with the exception of OB-MC. It could be that some part of these residual correlations is traceable to the fact that I have used very simple models with only two distance and contact variables. In particular, part of the residual correlation in the father-oldest brother model might possibly be incorporated into the direct effects of contact between oldest brother and father (a variable which has not been measured) on the other two contact variables. A model is presented in Appendix E which tests this hypothesis by making assumptions about the symmetric nature of the processes of contact in the case of respondent and father and of respondent's brother and father. Although the model suffers from defects and some variables are missing, it does demonstrate that direct effects of the three contact variables on one another are negligible, and that the observed positive correlations among the variables are left unexplained by the variables that were included. These observed correlations suggest that, aside from direct effects of the contact variables on one another, the two variables have other factors in common, such as family orientation or generalized sociability, or any of a number of other variables. A more prosaic but equally important possibility is that the questionnaire's posing of a series of questions about one relative, followed by the same series about a second relative may have caused an unrealistic correlation of responses. In this case, however, we might wonder why there is no such correlation in the OB-MC model.

Further research should aim to incorporate indicators of other relevant variables directly in the models and should also analyze systems larger than simple pair relationships. With the present data this was impossible, owing to the extremely small number of respondents for whom there were available data on distance and contact between three relatives, none of whom lived in the same city and none of whom lived in respondent's city. It is unreasonable to think of kinship behavior as interdependent in respect only to pair-wise behavior, however; and for that reason alone, aside from other reasons mentioned above, the models presented here are unrealistic. It is to be hoped that they do serve to demonstrate the potential complexity involved in the constructing of models which adequately explain kin contact, to say nothing of other aspects of behavior toward kinfolk.

FOOTNOTES

[1] He later conducts a multiple classification analysis of average number of visits per week with all relatives in the Detroit area, which shows that the location and existence of wife's mother is the most important single casual factor. However, his coefficients, which show a monotonic decline as distance from mother increases in three categories outside the respondent's household but a slight upturn in the "mother dead" category, lead one to suspect that the dependent variable is heavily weighted by visits with parents (i.e., mother), and the set of categories for location and existence of mother is important because it actually measures distance from mother.

[2] I had to assume, since I do not know the distance between relatives, that if both father and brother live an equal (nonzero) distance from respondent, then they live in the same city.

[3] A single slope for distance was included in the model because an F-test indicated that it was unnecessary to include separate distance slopes for the categories in which brother lives outside respondent's city (categories 2, 3, 4, and 7). The F-ratio is based on a comparison of models 1 and 2 in Appendix C. $F = .518$; $F_{.05}$ $(n_1 = 3, n_2 = 336) \doteq 2.65$.

[4] Regarding mother's oldest brother and father's oldest brother, category 7 has been eliminated, since there were only three of the one and two of the other. Individuals in these categories were also eliminated from the samples. The N's of both grandparents were too small to use for any models in this chapter.

[5] These are actually respondents of whom the given relatives were all living and for whom data existed as to both distance and contact variables. In a few cases, where data on contact were missing, the individuals were eliminated, as were also those whose fathers were dead or for whom the other relative did not exist.

[6] It was impossible to include both ln distance from brother and ln distance from father in category 2, since the two are identical. I decided to consider this variable as distance from brother.

[7] This model is presented as equation 5 in Appendix C. An F-test for each relative indicated that it was unnecessary to allow separate coefficients (increments to the intercept) for the location of father, inside or outside respondent's city.

[8] For a recursive model such as that shown in Figure 5.1, a description of the method and conventions of path analysis can be found in Duncan (1966).

[9] See Duncan (1969) for a discussion of some of the possible constraints that can be used to make models of this general form identifiable. Although the general form of the model is the same as that treated by Duncan, the meaning is quite different, since Duncan uses this model to study two-wave, two-variable panel data.

[10] See Duncan, Haller and Portes' discussion of "just-identified" models (1968:123-125). They include a description of the procedure in solving models of the kind shown in Figure 5.2.

CHAPTER 6

SUMMARY AND CONCLUSIONS

Summary

It is appropriate to summarize the major findings of the present study before placing them in the context of related research and of as yet unanswered questions of theory.

The first chapter of the study is devoted to the development of a basic model of the relationship between residential distance and the frequency of contact between married men (the respondents) and their fathers in a random sample of the American population. The sample was dichotomized as to whether the respondent's relatives lived in the same city as he did, or elsewhere. An adequate model of the distance-contact relationship is particularly important because factors such as ethnicity, religion and social status, which are thought to affect frequency of contact, are also correlated with distance — and distance may be found to account for the effect upon contact which was improperly attributed to the other variables. In the present research distance is treated as a continuous variable, and the relationship between distance and parental contact is shown as taking the general pattern of stimulus and response in which the rate of change in contact for a change in residential distance is proportional to the distance.

In the second chapter, the proportional model used to represent the distance-contact relationship is refined, and the economic concept of elasticity (which is represented by the regression coefficient in the linear regression form of the proportional model) is used to test hypotheses about the differences in the bearing of distance on contact with relatives of various degrees. The hypothesis that contacts with genealogically closer kin will be more elastic (show a greater percentage change in contact for a percentage change in distance) is supported: contacts with father have the greatest elasticity, followed by those with brother, then brother-in-law, maternal and paternal grandfather, male cousin, and maternal and paternal uncles. That the elasticities differ systematically by genealogical distance implies that people do distinguish between categories of relatives: even outside the family of procreation the relatives are not considered as undifferentiated individuals.

The hypothesis that there is a greater element of choice in contacts with genealogically more distant relatives may be taken to mean that visits with them are less predictable than visits with more intimate kin. The data support this hypothesis: the variance in contact explained by distance decreases according to increasing genealogical distance. When tested, an alternative interpretation — that, given equal access to various categories of relatives respondents are more variable in their contacts with more distantly related kin, because the pertinent norms are weaker — leads to the conclusion that there are no widely shared norms to prescribe the frequency of contact with any categories of kin. That different interpretations of the hypothesis of choice may lead to different conclusions demonstrates the need to be operationally specific in hypotheses about kinship behavior.

The third chapter examines the effects of occupational status and mobility on contact with parents by the technique of multiple classification analysis. The only major difference by occupational status is that between farmers and nonfarmers, the former being in more frequent contact with parents. This is because, as between farmers and nonfarmers living in the same city as their parents, the farmers live closer to them. The possibility that this is due to a difference in distance cannot be ruled out and indeed is strengthened by the fact that there is no difference in parental contact between nonfarmers with farm backgrounds and those with nonfarm backgrounds. Moreover, farmers see their parents more often because they live closer to them, not because of tradition. This finding supports the argument that industrialization reduces the individual's contact with his family of orientation, for industrialization brings about a decline in the proportion of farmers in the population, and the movement away from farms increases the average distance between offspring and their parents.

The literature leads to the expectation that blue-collar workers see their parents oftener, if only because they live closer to them; but actually lower white-collar respondents live closer to their parents and see more of them than either of the blue-collar categories. None of the various hypotheses about the effects of occupational mobility can be demonstrated to be valid.

Chapter 4 carries the analysis further by examining the effects of ethnicity, religion, city size, region, and age of respondents and their fathers on the frequency of visiting fathers. Only ethnicity and age still affect contact after differences in distance are taken into account. The Irish and Scandinavians are in the most frequent contact with their parents — a finding which contradicts the expectation that immigrants of the later waves of immigration, and particularly Italians, would score highest on contact because of their strong family structure in the homeland. A tentative explanation is that the more assimilated — such as Irish and Scandinavians — have had a longer time to develop a sturdy family structure in this country or did not originally meet with the extreme economic and social discrimination which undermined the stability of Southern European and nonwhite families. At this point in research, conditions of life and family structure in the country of ethnic origin appear to be less important than the length of time spent in the United States and/or the economic and social realities faced by various immigrant groups.[1]

Age affects contact only in the case of husbands in the same city as their fathers; and it is an effect of husband's, not father's age—a finding which implies that the constraints and opportunities in the husband's situation are more important in determining visits than are those in his father's. The age effect is nonmonotonic, with the youngest and oldest respondents scoring the most frequent contact. The possibility that this is due to the greater likelihood that the youngest and oldest respondents live in the same household as the parents is strongly though indirectly supported when the expected frequencies are adjusted for the probability of having living parents residing with the respondents. The lack of influence of age on husbands outside the city of father suggests that the visits of these sons have a meaning different from those of the sons who live nearby: husbands outside the city are unavailable to keep in close contact with elderly parents, and their visits are likely to be more sporadic and less affected by life-cycle or age differences.

Other variables, particularly religion and region, have sizeable indirect effects on parental contact. Roman Catholics live closer and, therefore, visit more frequently than do members of any other religious group; Westerners live further away from parents and, therefore, visit less frequently than others do. These variables lose their effect when distance is controlled.

Models are developed in the fifth chapter to test hypotheses about the interdependence of contacts with various relatives. According to regression models, neither the existence of nor the location of the father affects contacts with other relatives. However, the frequency of contact with father positively affects its frequency with other relatives. The frequency of contact with various relatives may be conceptualized as a measure of the demand for (contacts with) other relatives and the demands may be regarded as either complementary to or competitive with one another, in a manner analogous to commodities in a market. Simple demand models based on this conceptualization show that contacts with pairs of relatives have sizeable residual intercorrelations, although the direct effects of the contact variables on one another are usually negligible. The introduction of other variables not presently available (such as indicators of a family orientation, for example) would be required to explain this residual correlation.

Despite the limited nature of the exploration of this aspect of kinship behavior, it is hoped that the conceptual framework and the techniques employed here, as well as the substantive findings themselves, may prove useful to future research in this and related areas.

Concluding Remarks

The basic question asked in this study is: How isolated are people from their relatives? There are many ways to seek an answer, as the relevant theoretical and empirical literature will show. To begin with, an important distinction can be made between social isolation and structural isolation.

Recent literature, the present monograph included, focuses on the social isolation of the nuclear family, measuring it in terms of such variables as the frequency of actual interaction with kinfolk, participation in activities with them, the performing of regular services for them, and so on. Some of this literature (Sussman and Burchinal, 1962, for example) attempts to demonstrate that the nuclear family is not as socially isolated as earlier writers, notably Talcott Parsons (1954), claims. Although valuable in its own right, the literature misses at least two vital aspects of Parsons' orientation: (1) he was primarily interested in the structural isolation of the nuclear family, and (2) his perspective was both comparative and historical.[2]

By structure, Parsons was referring to the significant roles in the kinship system and the institutionalized relationships among them—that is, relationships and the expectations about the rights and duties involved in them, which are supported by either law or custom. In contrast to purely social ties, these relationships are not dependent on individual choice or the unique history of particular ones. A law of primogeniture, for example, is a structural link between the male lines of succeeding generations: it does not depend on the sentimental or emotional ties between particular fathers and sons. Similarly, laws or customs specifying which families or groups of families may intermarry are structural links between them. It is precisely the absence of such structural links which leads Parsons to conclude that the American family is structurally isolated: there are few institutionalized expectations about its members outside the immediate nuclear family or family of procreation.

Of course, the distinction between structural and social relationships is not always clear-cut; voluntary or specific ties can shade over into institutionalized ones if custom becomes strong enough, as it often is in cultural subgroups. The expectation of familial aid in emergencies might be an example of a borderline case; but even then there is no specified category of relatives that is expected to rise to the occasion. One can build an effective kinship network by selecting certain relatives arbitrarily, according to preference or propinquity. This is quite different from the prescriptions and proscriptions attached to categories of relationships in certain other societies.

Furthermore, structure has several meanings; and Parsons does not distinguish between them. There is the normative structure or system of institutionalized expectations just discussed, and there is also the structure of terminologically recognized roles in a kinship system—the taxonomy of kinship relations. Still another meaning of structure which Parsons sometimes makes use of is as the organization of functionally significant activities or patterns of behavior—that is, activities that have consequences upon other elements in the social system (when, for example, he speaks of preferential mating on a kinship basis as being "without structural significance" in this country). This last meaning emphasizes the interdependence of behavioral or normative patterns, rather than merely their terminological differentiation on some, usually implicit, criterion other than functional distinctiveness and interdependence.[3] Despite the overlapping problems of the social and structural isolation of kin and the multiple meanings of structure, the distinction is still useful for distinguishing between various traditions and problems of research.

Social Isolation

The concept of social isolation holds out several suggestions for further research, many of which have been demonstrated by the limitations of this study. A problem basic to any research is that of sampling—what is the population to which findings are being generalized, and how large a sample is necessary for it to be done with reasonable confidence? The present study makes use of a random sample of the population of the United States which, is obviously inadequate to the study of variation within certain cities. It is quite possible that factors explaining variation in social isolation within a city differ from those explaining variation in a national sample, since the composition of any given sample determines what factors are operating in it. However, an abnormally constituted city may be historically and functionally so different from others of its size as to render generalization unsafe.

Many of the hypotheses in the sociological literature on kinship refer to very small, particular groups which cannot be isolated in a simple random sample of the population. Hypotheses about the kinship structure and practices of the very rich are of this nature. Those who are seriously interested in examining these hypotheses must use either extremely large samples or stratified random samples in order to obtain the necessary representation. Furthermore, a sample which is homogeneous as regards some characteristic may tell nothing about the effect of variation in the characteristic. Thus, nothing may be inferred about socioeconomic differences in kinship from a sample composed entirely of well-to-do upper-class individuals. If, instead of a stratified random sample of the total population, the sample is of a population known to contain a disproportionate number of wealthy people (e.g., a wealthy suburb), then even the wealthy element there may turn out to be quite distinct from those in the national population, since they have chosen to live in a homogeneous wealthy suburb.

The present study has been limited to one measure of social interaction—the simple frequency of contact with kin. Even this measure has limitations (see Chapter 1). The original question asked about each male relative was, "How often do you see him?" and answers were given in categories which were converted to approximate annual frequencies. Obviously, there is a certain amount of inaccuracy in this reporting (which is one reason why it is possible to explain so much more variance in the log of frequency of contact than in the frequency itself), but also memories are unreliable, so that further refinement might be impossible over this span of time. On relatives who are seen regularly it might be useful to get more detailed data covering a shorter interval—say, the week before the interview. However, any question on contacts in a specific short period, such as a week, turns that period into a sample of all the weeks in a year. Such a sample is sure to be biased by the season, the weather and other circumstances.[4] Repeated interviews in different weeks would be ideal but expensive. The investigators would also be plagued by the usual problems of nonresponse in longitudinal studies.

Another serious limitation of the present study is the lack of any measure either to distinguish contacts of various kinds or to determine who initiates them. Different kinds of contacts undoubtedly have different meaning to the participants. If familial duties are felt, then an invitation to a daughter and her family for dinner must have greater significance for the discharging of obligations than does a casual conversation with her in the afternoon. The personal investment of time and creative energy is certainly much greater in the former than in the latter.

The size of the investment upon relatives of time and energy is an important dimension along which a taxonomy of types of familial interaction could be constructed. This or some other taxonomy is urgently needed, for in its absence it is impossible to attach meaning to the various forms of kinship behavior. A reliable scale to distinguish activities according to how far they go toward fulfilling kinship obligations or representing the commitment of one relative to the other would be extremely useful for differentiating types of relationships and the strength of kinship and friendship ties.[5] Such a scale would have to make quite refined distinctions between relationships which are subtly different from one another. Furthermore, the actions which demonstrate commitment in one subculture or social class may not be the same as those in another. For example, taking relatives out to dinner costs more but requires less time and thought than inviting them for dinner; and which is considered to be a greater investment depends on how highly money and time are valued and whether substituting them is considered acceptable. In some subcultures such a trade-off would be permissible; in others, not. Whether friends are invited together with relatives is also a subtle and important distinction, indicating to the relatives their place in the hierarchy of voluntary association of the host and hostess or the latter's willingness to sacrifice conventional criteria for the sake of the kinship tie.

The differentiation of kinship behavior is also important in the study of historical change in the interdependence of relatives. Social scientists who speculate on historical change in the isolation from kin may really have in mind changes in the services which kinsmen perform for one another. As I pointed out in the discussion of occupational effects, very few occupations remain in which members of a family can be directly useful to one another, so that one of the bases of frequent interaction of relatives has declined. Since farming is one occupation in which the extended family can be directly useful and since the proportion of farmers has fallen tremendously over the years, some of the decline in kinship orientation (if defined in terms of functional interdependence) may be attributed to this and other changes in the occupational distribution.

There are day-to-day needs, once met by members of the family which are increasingly being provided for by specialists and specialized institutions. Care of elderly parents, for instance, once considered a responsibility of adult offspring, is now being relegated more and more to institutions. Even here, however, it is a question whether a greater proportion of elderly parents are cared for by institutions or simply a greater number, since demographic changes have caused an increase in the number of elderly parents to be cared for. Institutions such as nursing homes could grow and thrive on an absolute increase in the number of their elderly patients, with or without a decline in the proportion being cared for by offspring.

In considering the hypothesis that the activities involved in kin contact have changed with time, one must also keep in mind that distance is an important covariate in the problem: that is, the services which members of the family can perform for one another must differ considerably with distance. Thus a grandmother who lives 500 miles away from her daughter can hardly be a regular babysitter. If the functions which the members perform for one another have changed, such changes are likely to show only if distance is included as a covariate, either in continuous or in categorical form. Furthermore, in the absence of information on the relationships among types of services or functions they perform for one another and the distances at which given functions can be performed, composite measures of "functional interdependence," may be made only at the risk of completely masking the effects of the individual items. One alternative is to treat the frequency (or the probability) of the performance of given functions or services or different kinds of contact as simultaneous dependent variables, subject to secular trends and the influence of distance.

Still another meaning of the hypothesis of the growing isolation of kinfolk is simply that they live farther apart than they once did. However, "farther apart" could have several meanings. If the location of families of orientation relative to that of families of procreation has indeed changed over the years it may be entirely due to the fact that the single nuclear family in its own household has become the dominant pattern, as Parsons (1954) claimed. Assuming that the family of orientation is less likely to continue living in the same household than it once was (and the probability varies with the stages of the life cycle), there may be no other change in the relative location of the two households. Then, too, the particular historical periods which are chosen to test the hypothesis may also affect the outcome, since it is possible that certain groups in certain periods (e.g., blacks during World Wars I and II or European immigrants in the periods of great immigration) experienced extensive migration which temporarily split the nuclear family apart or separated it from the family of orientation. These families may have coalesced again as soon as opportunities for doing so presented themselves.

Another complication is that the meaning of distance has changed with the advent of modern forms of transportation and communication and with increased relative affluence, so that even if the distance has not changed, the cost of visits, in terms of time or money or energy, may be relatively lower. If kinship isolation is defined in terms of frequency of contact, whether face-to-face or of some other kind, then it is possible that kin, especially those who do not live near each other, are less isolated from each other than they were previously, simply because they can afford it.

There is also the unanswered question of change in kinship behavior within the lifetime of given individuals. The present study assumes that in the short run the distance between kinfolk is fixed on the basis of prior decisions. Ideally, however, we should have personal histories covering occupation, migration, and contact, in order to sort out the actual causal relationships between the decision to leave home, to follow a certain career, and to maintain contact with parents. There are many possible causal sequences, and as they probably differ in different individuals, only longitudinal analysis can make clear which of them operate in a given case. It may be that to move away from the city of one's parents is a critical decision, explained by factors different from those which determine how far to go, once one has decided to leave home. The original decision to move may be caused by a crucial break with the family or with tradition, as, for example, being drafted into the military or marrying outside the faith). Given that residential distance is the most important factor in determining frequency of contact in the short run, we must explain what determines distance from relatives, particularly from parents. Residential distance has been shown to be correlated with farm-nonfarm, religious, ethnic and regional differences and with differences in size of city. However, to repeat, the meaning of these correlations cannot really be established without histories of migration.

Finally, any study which uses residential distance as either an independent or a dependent variable should profit from the weakness of this study by making sure that variation in distance is known between kinfolk who live in the same city as a given relative. Intra-city distances will have to be refined, since actual mileage is probably less important than transportation time and/or cost.

Structural Isolation

Concerning structural isolation the question arises: Is the American nuclear family structurally isolated from the family of orientation and other kin? And then, if so, how do we measure such isolation?

Some small-scale work has been done by anthropologists on the terminological aspect of kinship structure in the United States and Britain. See Codere (1955); Schneider and Homans (1955); Schneider (1968); Firth, Hubert and Forge (1969: Ch. 10). However, there is no study as yet that is based on a random sample of the national population, and no comparative work has yet been attempted, to my knowledge. Research would undoubtedly show considerable variation in just which kin are recognized either by terminology or by name in various families and subcultures. Such variation, however, may also exist in nonliterate societies and be overlooked simply because of reliance on one or a few informants. On a matter such as kinship terminology each interviewee can be considered as the equivalent of an informant on his own subculture.

The broader normative aspect of kinship structure and structural isolation can, of course, be studied by examining the laws found in cultures which have written laws. Parsons mentions inheritance laws (1954: 184); Farber (1968) compares kinship systems through analysis of the laws on first-cousin marriage. However, the law may be quite different from the patterns of behavior and norms that are actually followed. For example, when the survivors contest a will they are implicitly making statements about who ought to inherit property; and the decision of the court is another normative statement. Where wills are made public, the actual patterns of inheritance can be studied in the testaments themselves and compared to patterns in other countries. Thus, Parsons noted (1954: 184) that in our society there is "a relative weakness of pressure to leave all or even most property to kin." Whether this is actually true is open to question: it may be that the proportion left to kin decreases as the value of the property increases. Survivors may also express definite ideas about who ought to inherit property in their family—or who ought to have, but did not—provided there is anything to inherit. The discretionary nature of inheritance in the United States is itself a possible cause of the break in ties to the extended family. Everyone knows of at least one family one branch of which is not on speaking terms with another because of a dis-agreement over the inheritance of property. Although a large proportion of the population is not involved in such disputes, the latter should not be over-looked in the historical explanation of the loss of ties to kin in given families.[6]

Guest lists for weddings are another possible source of data on the nor-mative aspect of kinship structure. Weddings can be traced through marriage licenses, and where there is a willingness to divulge information about what guests were invited to weddings, a great deal may be learned about kinship obligations. In fact, the obligation or commitment involved in various re-lationships might be measured by whether a guest is invited to the reception only, to the wedding ceremony, to a wedding dinner, or to be actually a mem-ber of the wedding party. (One would, of course, have to take into account the size and elaborateness of the affair.) The relative proportions of friends and relatives invited to the wedding is also an indicator of the importance of kin, as is, too, the distance which people are expected to travel and their willingness to undertake the trip, distances being equal. These are but a few possibilities in the measurement of structural isolation and research on it.

The causes of structural isolation, which has often been regarded as an adaptation to industrialization and to an occupational system which requires great spatial mobility, deserve further study. The assumption that family structure has changed as a consequence of changes in the industrial system has been criticized on several grounds (for example, by Greenfield, 1961; and Furstenberg, 1966). Parsons (1954), however, does not argue a simple one-way causation between the occupational system and the kinship system; rather, he talks about a "process of mutual accommodation" (p. 192) be-tween an occupational system which requires that individuals be treated without regard to ascribed status and a kinship system which facilitates this prerequisite. Thus the kinship system may permit certain kinds of occupa-tional systems to develop, just as much as particular occupational systems may select kinship structures which can adapt to them and succeed in them. Furthermore, nothing in Parsons' essay requires the relationship between the two systems to be fixed—there may be constant readjustment between them.

The assumption of the demands for individualistic treatment on the basis of achieved criteria which lies at the heart of Parsons' argument is open to question and modification, however. While the family of orientation plays very little direct part in obtaining jobs, it may powerfully affect occupational decisions such as those about location, especially in certain groups. Con-straints on location, in turn, interfere with the quality of education and the available employment. Migration and job histories would be very useful in determining whether and when Parsons' assumption is valid.

Finally, what are the consequences of the structural isolation of American families? Parsons addresses himself to this question in his essay (1954), again from a comparative and historical perspective. In a sense, he is always look-ing at "intersocietal" and "intertemporal" variation, so that isolation is relative by comparison to other kinship systems. Those who argue against Parsons' position look only at variation *within* a single society—in fact, with-in a single community at a single point in time. They therefore do not really confront Parsons' major hypotheses. For example, Parsons proposes (1954: 187-188) that in highly interdependent kinship systems there is a tendency "to limit the scope of 'personal' emotional feeling or, at least, its direct expression in action" because "any considerable range of affective spontaneity would tend to impinge on the statuses and interests of too many others, with disequilibrating consequences for the system as a whole." Of course, the fact that something would have disequilibrating consequences is no assurance that it does not occur. Systems are not necessarily in equilibrium, and the existence of a disequilibrating mechanism might be an important agent of change. In any case, Parsons' argument implies that in structurally isolated systems, such as in the United States, people are free to express their affective inclinations in their actions.

Parsons further adds that affective devotion and subjective sentiments are likely to be a functional substitute for institutional supports where these are lacking—which means the two should be inversely related. The expression of affective sentiments in word and deed is most likely where there are no structural guarantees of stability. If so, then the interpretation of behavioral manifestations of kinship solidarity as reflecting the nature of the kinship structure (as defined here) is misguided. One would expect a particularly high level of behavioral manifestations of affective ties or social ties (such as liking, visiting, etc.) in precisely such a society as ours—and especially in the urban middle class—where there are least likely to be structural reasons for the interdependence of kin.

This hypothesis is only one of several involving the comparative analysis of kinship structures in modern societies which can be derived from Parsons' essay. I mention it here because it suggests a possible link between structural isolation and the social isolation which is the contemporary focus of sociologists. The nature of the relationship between the structural and social aspects of kinship, whatever it may turn out to be, is one which has been barely explored but which definitely merits investigation.

FOOTNOTES

[1]Lopreato (1970:98-99) makes a similar point in regard to Italian-Americans, when he criticizes Gans and others for seeming "oblivious to the possibility that much of Italian-American behavior has roots nowhere but in the American slum."

[2]Firth, Hubert and Forge (1969:457) also note that Parsons indicated that family studies at the time were "overwhelmingly oriented to problems of individual adjustment rather than to comparative structural perspective."

[3]This is what Duncan and Schnore refer to as "ecological structure" (1959:142); and their distinction between cultural, behavioral, and ecological perspectives may be usefully applied to the study of the family as well as to other units of social organization. The term "social" as I have been using it here would correspond to Duncan and Schnore's use of "behavioral." However, Parsons' use of "structural," which I am following, combines elements of both the cultural and ecological perspectives discussed by Duncan and Schnore, with the emphasis definitely on the cultural side.

[4]See Michelson's article (1971) for evidence of seasonal variation in the frequency of interaction with both friends and relatives.

[5]The ability to distinguish between types of relationship on the basis of the activities and the emotional investment involved in them would be directly relevant to the refinements of the distinction between *Gemeinschaft* and *Gesellschaft* made by Toennies, a distinction which was originally meant to apply to the intimacy of relationships. (See Toennies, 1961.)

[6]Firth, Hubert and Forge (1969:372-378) discuss in a qualitative fashion disputes over money in the families in their study.

DUMMY VARIABLES AND EQUATIONS USED IN MODELS PRESENTED IN CHAPTER 3

Dummy Variables

(On each dummy variable, a respondent is coded 1 if he is a member of the category listed; if not in the category, he is coded 0.)

X_1 — respondent lives in same city as father

X_2 — respondent lives outside city of father

X_3 — upper white-collar respondent

X_4 — lower white-collar respondent

X_5 — upper blue-collar respondent

X_6 — lower blue-collar respondent

X_7 — farm respondent

X_8 — nonfarm respondent

X_9 — upper white-collar father

X_{10} — lower white-collar father

X_{11} — upper blue-collar father

X_{12} — lower blue-collar father

X_{13} — farm father

X_{14} — nonfarm father

X_{15} — nonfarm respondent with farm father [Cells (5,1) (5,2) (5,3) (5,4)]*

X_{16} — nonfarm respondent with nonfarm father [Cells (1,1) (1,2) (1,3) (1,4) (2,1) (2,2) (2,3) (2,4) (3,1) (3,2) (3,3) (3,4) (4,1) (4,2) (4,3) (4,4)]*

X_{17} — mobile [Cells (1,2) (1,3) (1,4) (1,5) (2,1) (2,3) (2,4) (2,5) (3,1) (3,2) (3,4) (3,5) (4,1) (4,2) (4,3) (4,5)]*

X_{18} — stable [Cells (1,1) (2,2) (3,3) (4,4) (5,5)]*

X_{19} — upwardly mobile [Cells (2,1) (3,1) (3,2) (4,1) (4,2) (4,3) (5,1) (5,2) (5,3) (5,4)]*

*Cells refer to cells in Figure 3.1 in text.

X_{20} — downwardly mobile [Cells (1,2) (1,3) (1,4) (1,5) (2,3) (2,4) (2,5) (3,4) (3,5) (4,5)]*

X_{21} — extremely mobile [Cells (1,3) (1,4) (1,5) (2,4) (2,5) (3,1) (3,5) (4,1) (4,2) (5,1) (5,3) (5,4)]*

X_{22} — stable or not extremely mobile [Cells (1,1) (1,2) (2,1) (2,2) (2,3) (3,2) (3,3) (3,4) (4,3) (4,4) (4,5) (5,4) (5,5)]*

X_{23} — extremely upwardly mobile [Cells (3,1) (4,1) (4,2) (5,1) (5,2) (5,3)]*

X_{24} — extremely downwardly mobile [Cells (1,3) (1,4) (1,5) (2,4) (2,5) (3,5)]*

Equations

The following equations are presented in the form in which regressions were computed in order to make it easier for the reader to determine the proper number of degrees of freedom for F-tests used in the text and to determine which variables in linearly dependent sets have been omitted in order to obtain a regression solution. The transformation of regression coefficients to the MCA coefficients used in the text is a simple one, described in Melichar (1965).

1. $\ln \widehat{C}_i = b_0 + b_1 X_{2i} + \sum_{j=2}^{5} b_j X_{j+1_i} X_{1i} + \sum_{j=6}^{9} b_j X_{j-3_i} X_{2i} + \sum_{j=10}^{13} b_j X_{j-1_i} X_{1i}$

   $+ \sum_{j=14}^{17} b_j X_{j-5_i} X_{2i} + b_{18} \ln D_i$

2. $\ln \widehat{C}_i = b_0 + b_1 X_{2i} + b_2 \ln D_i$

3. $\ln \widehat{C}_i = b_0 + b_1 X_{2i} + \sum_{j=2}^{5} b_j X_{j+1_i} + \sum_{j=6}^{9} b_j X_{j+3_i} + b_{10} \ln D_i$

4. $\ln \widehat{C}_i = b_0 + b_1 X_{2i} + b_2 X_{8i} X_{1i} + b_3 X_{8i} X_{2i} + b_4 \ln D_i$

5. $\ln \widehat{C}_i = b_0 + b_0 X_{2i} + \sum_{j=2}^{4} b_j X_{j+1_i} X_{1i} + \sum_{j=5}^{7} b_j X_{j-2_i} X_{2i} + \sum_{j=8}^{11} b_j X_{j+1_i} X_{1i}$

   $+ \sum_{j=12}^{15} b_j X_{j-3_i} X_{2i} + b_{16} \ln D_i$

6. $\ln \widehat{C}_i = b_0 + b_1 X_{2i} + \sum_{j=2}^{4} b_j X_{j+1_i} + \sum_{j=5}^{8} b_j X_{j+4_i} + b_9 \ln D_i$

7. $\ln \widehat{C}_i = b_0 + b_1 X_{8i} X_{1i} + b_2 X_{7i} X_{1i} + b_3 X_{8i} X_{2i}$

8. $\ln \widehat{C}_i = b_0 + b_1 X_{2i} + b_2 X_{8i} X_{1i} + b_3 \ln D_i$

9. $\ln \widehat{C}_i = b_0 + b_1 X_{2i} + b_2 X_{8i} + b_3 \ln D_i$

10. $\ln \widehat{C}_i = b_0 + b_1 X_{2i} + b_2 X_{15i} X_{1i} + b_3 X_{16i} X_{1i} + b_4 X_{15i} X_{2i} + b_5 X_{16i} X_{2i}$
    $\quad + b_6 \ln D_i$

11. $\ln \widehat{C}_i = b_0 + b_1 X_{2i} + b_2 X_{17i} X_{1i} + b_3 X_{17i} X_{2i} + b_4 \ln D_i$

12. $\ln \widehat{C}_i = b_0 + b_1 X_{2i} + b_2 X_{17i} + b_3 \ln D_i$

13. $\ln \widehat{C}_i = b_0 + b_1 X_{2i} + b_2 X_{19i} X_{1i} + b_3 X_{20i} X_{1i} + b_4 X_{19i} X_{2i} + b_5 X_{20i} X_{2i}$
    $\quad + b_6 \ln D_i$

14. $\ln \widehat{C}_i = b_0 + b_1 X_{2i} + b_2 X_{19i} + b_3 X_{20i} + b_4 \ln D_i$

15. $\ln \widehat{C}_i = b_0 + b_1 X_{2i} + b_2 X_{21i} X_{1i} + b_3 X_{21i} X_{2i} + b_4 \ln D_i$

16. $\ln \widehat{C}_i = b_0 + b_1 X_{2i} + b_2 X_{21i} + b_3 \ln D_i$

17. $\ln \widehat{C}_i = b_0 + b_1 X_{2i} + b_2 X_{23i} X_{1i} + b_3 X_{24i} X_{1i} + b_4 X_{23i} X_{2i} + b_5 X_{24i} X_{2i}$
    $\quad + b_6 \ln D_i$

18. $\ln \widehat{C}_i = b_0 + b_1 X_{2i} + b_2 X_{23i} + b_3 X_{24i} + b_4 \ln D_i$

DUMMY VARIABLES AND EQUATIONS USED IN MODELS PRESENTED IN CHAPTER 4

Dummy Variables

(On each dummy variable a respondent is coded 1 if he is a member of the category listed; if not in the category, he is coded 0.)

X_1 — respondent lives in same city as father
X_2 — respondent lives outside city of father
X_3 — Irish
X_4 — Scandinavian
X_5 — German, Dutch, Swiss
X_6 — Eastern European
X_7 — Nonwhite and Other
X_8 — English, Scottish, and U.S.A. White
X_9 — French, Italian, Spanish
X_{10} — Baptist
X_{11} — Episcopalian, Presbyterian, Lutheran
X_{12} — Methodist, Congregational
X_{13} — Other Protestant
X_{14} — Roman Catholic
X_{15} — Jewish, Other, No Religion
X_{16} — SMA's of 2,000,000 or more
X_{17} — SMA's of 50,000-2,000,000
X_{18} — Cities and Towns 10,000-50,000
X_{19} — Counties with No Towns as Large as 10,000
X_{20} — Northeast
X_{21} — North Central
X_{22} — South

X23 — West
X24 — Husband's Age 15-24
X25 — Husband's Age 25-34
X26 — Husband's Age 35-44
X27 — Husband's Age 45-64
X28 — Father's Age 35-54
X29 — Father's Age 55-64
X30 — Father's Age 65-74
X31 — Father's Age 75 and over

Equations

The following equations are presented in the form in which regressions were computed in order to make it easier for the reader to determine the proper number of degrees of freedom for F-tests used in the text and to determine which variables in linearly dependent sets have been omitted in order to obtain a regression solution. The transformation of regression coefficients to the MCA coefficients used in the text is a simple one, described in Melichar (1965).

1. $\ln \hat{C}_i = b_0 + b_1 X_{2i} + \sum_{j=2}^{7} b_j X_{j+1_i} X_{1i} + \sum_{j=8}^{13} b_j X_{j-5_i} X_{2i} + b_{14} \ln D_i$

2. $\ln \hat{C}_i = b_0 + b_1 X_{2i} + \sum_{j=2}^{7} b_j X_{j+1_i} + b_8 \ln D_i$

3. $\ln \hat{C}_i = b_0 + \sum_{j=1}^{6} b_j X_{j+2_i}$

4. $\ln \hat{C}_i = b_0 + b_1 X_{2i} + b_2 \ln D_i$

5. $\ln \hat{C}_i = b_0 + b_1 X_{2i} + \sum_{j=2}^{6} b_j X_{j+8_i} X_{1i} + \sum_{j=7}^{11} b_j X_{j+3_i} X_{2i} + b_{12} \ln D_i$

6. $\ln \hat{C}_i = b_0 + b_1 X_{2i} + \sum_{j=2}^{6} b_j X_{j+8i} + b_7 \ln D_i$

7. $\ln \hat{C}_i = b_0 + \sum_{j=1}^{5} b_j X_{j+9_i}$

8. $\ln \hat{C}_i = b_0^{\cdot} + b_1 X_{2i} + \sum_{j=2}^{7} b_j X_{j+1_i} + \sum_{j=8}^{12} b_j X_{j+2_i} + b_{13} \ln D_i$

9. $\ln \hat{C}_i = b_0 + b_1 X_{2i} + \sum_{j=2}^{4} b_j X_{j+14_i} X_{1i} + \sum_{j=5}^{7} b_j X_{j+11_i} X_{2i} + b_8 \ln D_i$

10. $\ln \hat{C}_i = b_0 + b_1 X_{2i} + \sum_{j=2}^{4} b_j X_{j+14_i} + b_5 \ln D_i$

11. $\ln \widehat{C}_i = b_0 + \sum_{j=1}^{3} b_j X_{j+15_i}$

12. $\ln \widehat{C}_i = b_0 + b_1 X_{2i} + \sum_{j=2}^{4} b_j X_{j+18_i} X_{1i} + \sum_{j=5}^{7} b_j X_{j+15_i} X_{2i} + b_8 \ln D_i$

13. $\ln \widehat{C}_i = b_0 + b_1 X_{2i} + \sum_{j=2}^{4} b_j X_{j+18_i} + b_5 \ln D_i$

14. $\ln \widehat{C}_i = b_0 + \sum_{j=1}^{3} b_j X_{j+19_i}$

15. $\ln \widehat{C}_i = b_0 + b_1 X_{2i} + \sum_{j=2}^{4} b_j X_{j+22_i} X_{1i} + \sum_{j=5}^{7} b_j X_{j+19_i} X_{2i} + \sum_{j=8}^{10} b_j X_{j+20_i} X_{1i}$

$+ \sum_{j+11}^{13} b_j X_{j+17_i} X_{2i} + b_{14} \ln D_i$

16. $\ln \widehat{C}_i = b_0 + b_1 X_{2i} + \sum_{j=2}^{4} b_j X_{j+22_i} + \sum_{j=5}^{7} b_j X_{j+23_i} + b_8 \ln D_i$

17. $\ln \widehat{C}_i = b_0 + b_1 X_{2i} + \sum_{j=2}^{4} b_j X_{j+22_i} X_{1i} + \sum_{j=5}^{7} b_j X_{j+19_i} X_{2i} + b_8 \ln D_i$

18. $\ln \widehat{C}_i = b_0 + b_1 X_{2i} + \sum_{j=2}^{4} b_j X_{j+22_i} X_{1i} + b_5 \ln D_i$

19. $\ln \widehat{C}_i = b_0 + b_1 X_{2i} + \sum_{j=2}^{7} b_j X_{j+1_i} + \sum_{j=8}^{10} b_j X_{j+16_i} X_{1i} + b_{11} \ln D_i$

DUMMY VARIABLES AND EQUATIONS USED IN MODELS PRESENTED IN CHAPTER 5

Dummy Variables

(On each dummy variable a respondent is coded 1 if he is a member of the category listed; if not in the category he is coded 0.)

X_1 — father and other relative live in same city as respondent

X_2 — father and other relative live in same city; neither in respondent's city

X_3 — father and other relative live in different cities; neither lives in respondent's city

X_4 — father lives in respondent's city; other relative lives in different city

X_5 — other relative lives in respondent's city; father lives in a different city

X_6 — father dead; other relative lives in respondent's city

X_7 — father dead; other relative lives in a different city

X_8 — other relative lives in respondent's city

X_9 — other relative lives outside respondent's city

X_{10} — father is alive

X_{11} — father lives in respondent's city

X_{12} — father lives outside respondent's city

Equations (Using oldest brother as example of "other relative")

The following equations are presented in the form in which regressions were computed in order to make it easier for the reader to determine the proper number of degrees of freedom for F-tests used in the text and to determine which variables in linearly dependent sets have been omitted in order to obtain a regression solution. The transformation of regression coefficients to the MCA coefficients used in the text is a simple one, described in Melichar (1965).

Note: For Equations 1 through 4, $\sum_{j=1}^{7} X_{ji} = 1$. For Equations 5 through 8, $\sum_{j=1}^{5} X_{ji} = 1$, since the members of categories 6 and 7 were eliminated.

1. $\ln \widehat{C}_i^{OB} = b_0 + \sum_{j=1}^{6} b_j X_{ji} + b_7 X_{2i} \ln D_i^{OB} + b_8 X_{3i} \ln D_i^{OB} + b_9 X_{4i} \ln D_i^{OB}$

   $\qquad + b_{10} X_{7i} \ln D_i^{OB} + b_{11} X_{9i}$

2. $\ln \widehat{C}_i^{OB} = b_0 + \sum_{j=1}^{6} b_j X_{ji} + b_7 X_{9i} \ln D_i^{OB} + b_8 X_{9i}$

3. $\ln \widehat{C}_i^{OB} = b_0 + b_1 X_{9i} \ln D_i^{OB} + b_2 X_{9i}$

4. $\ln \widehat{C}_i^{OB} = b_0 + b_1 X_{9i} \ln D_i^{OB} + b_2 X_{9i} + b_3 X_{10i}$

5. $\ln \widehat{C}_i^{OB} = b_0 + b_1 X_{9i} + b_2 X_{9i} \ln D_i^{OB} + b_3 X_{12i} \ln D_i^{F} + b_4 \ln C_i^{F}$

6. $\ln \widehat{C}_i^{OB} = b_0 + \sum_{j=1}^{4} b_j X_{ji} + b_5 X_{2i} \ln D_i^{OB} + b_6 X_{3i} \ln D_i^{OB} + b_7 X_{4i} \ln D_i^{OB}$

   $\qquad + b_8 X_{3i} \ln D_i^{F} + b_9 X_{5i} \ln D_i^{F} + \sum_{j=10}^{14} b_j X_{j-9_i} \ln C_i^{F} + b_{15} X_{8i}$

7. $\ln \widehat{C}_i^{OB} = b_0 + b_1 X_{9i} \ln D_i^{OB} + b_3 \ln C_i^{F}$

8. $\ln \widehat{C}_i^{OB} = b_0 + b_1 X_{9i} + b_2 X_{9i} \ln D_i^{OB} + b_3 X_{12i} \ln D_i^{F}$

APPENDIX D

N's OF PAIRS OF RELATIVES IN VARIOUS CATEGORIES OF EXISTENCE OF FATHER AND LOCATION OF FATHER AND OTHER RELATIVE

Categories of Location and Father's Existence	Pairs of Relatives				
	F-OB	F-HOMS	F-MC	F-FOB	F-MOB
1. Father and Relative Live in Same City as Respondent	46	34	47	23	20
2. Father and Relative Live in Same City; Neither in Respondent's City.*	20	21	19	11	19
3. Father and Relative Live in Different Cities; Neither in Respondent's City.	42	36	58	31	45
4. Father Lives in Respondent's City; Relative Lives in Different City	14	20	53	28	39
5. Relative Lives in Respondent's City; Father Lives in Different City	6	11	14	—	—
6. Father Dead; Relative Lives in Respondent's City	88	66	96	14	21
7. Father Dead; Relative Lives in Different City	131	126	212	38	78
Total	347	314	499	145	222

*If both father and other relative live the same distance from respondent, they are assumed to live in the same city. See footnote 2 in Chapter 5.

APPENDIX E

AN ADDITIONAL MODEL OF INTERDEPENDENCE OF THE CONTACTS

The path diagram in Figure E.1 represents a tentative model of the causal relationships among distance and contacts among three relatives—respondent (R), father (F), and brother (B). It includes parameters for the effects of ln distance in the case of each pair of relatives (if the two are in different cities) on their ln contact and a coefficient for the dummy variable representing same city, if they live in the same city. It also includes parameters for the effects of each of the three simultaneously dependent contact variables on one another. The variable descriptions and symbols are listed below.

Variables

D_1 — ln distance between F and R if neither in same city.
S_1 — dummy variable, equals 1 if both F and R in same city; equas 0 otherwise.
C_1 — ln contact between F and R.
D_2 — ln distance between B and R if neither in same city.
S_2 — dummy variable, equals 1 if both B and R in same city; equals 0 otherwise.
C_2 — ln contact between B and R.
D_3 — ln distance between F and B if in same city.
S_3 — dummy variable, equals 1 if both F and B in same city; equals 0 otherwise.
C_3 — ln contact between B and F.

A Model to Represent Contact Among Three Relatives

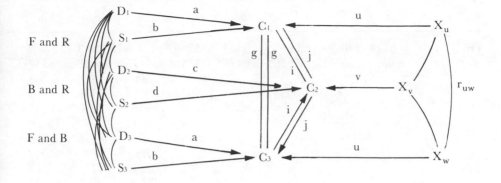

This would ordinarily be an overidentified model, since there are four causal variables for each endogenous variable, while there are six predetermined variables in the model. The parameters for such a model could be estimated by a two-stage least squares procedure (see Duncan, 1968 and 1970). In the present case, however, we do not know the values of either D_3 or C_3—ln distance and ln contacts between brother and father. We do know S_3, since I assumed earlier that if F and B live an equal distance from R, then they live in the same city (see footnote 2 in Chapter V). In the absence of these variables, the model as it stands is underidentified.

I have been able to estimate the (standardized) parameters of this model, however, by assuming symmetry in the contacts of respondent with father and brother with father. The justification of this assumption is that in the survey the choice of respondent or the oldest brother (who, it will be recalled, may or may not be older than respondent) as interviewee was at random. That is, the designation of one of the two as "oldest brother" rather than "respondent" is due only to the fact that it is the latter who was interviewed. On the basis of this symmetry, comparable coefficients in the model are assumed identical (see Figure E.1); and correlations between D_3 and C_3 with D_2, S_2, and C_2 are assumed equal to correlations of the latter with D_1 and C_1, respectively. The assumed correlations are denoted in Table E.1 by pairs of variables in parentheses, indicating the source of the correlation.

The assumption of symmetry can be checked by comparing three correlations for which I do have observed values:

$r_{S_3 D_2}$ (–.5907), which should equal $r_{S_1 D_2}$ (–.5912)

$r_{S_3 S_2}$ (.6140), which should equal $r_{S_1 S_2}$ (.6811)

$r_{S_3 C_2}$ (.4171), which should equal $r_{S_1 C_2}$ (.4326)

The similarity of the members of these pairs of correlations does inspire confidence in the assumption of symmetry of contacts between F and R and contacts

Correlations for Model Presented in Figure E.1 for 125 Male Respondents

	D_1	S_1	C_1	D_2	S_2	C_2	D_3	S_3	C_3
D_1	x	−.8724	−.8614	.6680	−.5973	−.5256	—	−.4149	—
S_1		x	.6789	−.5910*	.6478*	.4248*	−.4149 (S_3D_1)	.4738	.3339 (C_1S_3)
C_1			x	−.6053	.4839	.6027	—	.3339	—
D_2				x	−.8695	−.7597	.6680 (D_1D_2)	−.5910*	−.6053 (C_1D_2)
S_2					x	.6083	−.5973 (D_1S_2)	.6478*	.4839 (C_1S_2)
C_2						x	−.5256 (D_1C_2)	.4248*	.6027 (C_1C_2)
D_3							x	−.8724 (S_1D_1)	−.8614 (C_1D_1)
S_3								x	.6789 (C_1S_1)
C_3									x

*These correlations are averages of the pairs of correlations discussed in the text.

between F and B. These pairs of correlations have been averaged to obtain the appropriate correlations in Table E.1.

To obtain the path coefficients a, b, j and g, I multiplied Equation 1, which follows, through by each of the predetermined variables.

Equation 1. $C_1 = aD_1 + bS_1 + jC_2 + gC_3 + uX_u$

The six equations obtained are presented below, since they are useful in explaining how the coefficients were derived.

1A. $r_{C_1D_1} = a + br_{S_1D_1} + jr_{C_2D_1} + gr_{C_3D_1} + ur_{X_uD_1}$

1B. $r_{C_1S_1} = ar_{D_1S_1} + b + jr_{C_2S_1} + gr_{C_3S_1}$

1C. $r_{C_1D_2} = ar_{D_1D_2} + br_{S_1D_2} + jr_{C_2D_2} + gr_{C_3D_2}$

1D. $r_{C_1S_2} = ar_{D_1S_2} + br_{S_1S_2} + jr_{C_2S_2} + gr_{C_3S_2}$

1E. $r_{C_1D_3} = ar_{D_1D_3} + br_{S_1D_3} + jr_{C_2D_3} + gr_{C_3D_3} + ur_{X_uD_3}$

1F. $r_{C_1S_3} = ar_{D_1S_3} + br_{S_1S_3} + jr_{C_3S_3} + gr_{C_3S_3}$

Note that we have required four correlations of residuals with predetermined variables to be zero. This assumption is necessary to obtain a solution. Although there are only four unknowns, there are also only four usable equations; Equations 1A and 1E involve the unknown correlations $r_{C_3 D_1}$ and $r_{D_1 D_3}$ and cannot be used. I therefore estimated the coefficients by inverting the matrix based on the four equations 1B, 1C, 1D and 1F. In doing so I obtain parameter estimates which are consistent but not necessarily the most efficient estimates. All of the standardized coefficients are listed below, although I have not yet explained how c, d, and i were obtained.

$$a = -1.3236 \qquad c = -.9261 \qquad j = -.0169 \qquad i = .0131$$
$$b = -.4776 \qquad d = -.2096 \qquad g = .0263$$

These estimates are based on the same sample of respondents with living fathers for whom distance and contact data were present (N = 125).

The three coefficients c, d, and i were obtained by multiplying Equation 2 through by each of the predetermined variables.

Equation 2. $C_2 = cD_2 + dS_2 + iC_1 + iC_3 + vX_v$

The six equations obtained are:

2A. $r_{C_2 D_1} = cr_{D_2 D_1} + dr_{S_2 D_1} + ir_{C_1 D_1} + ir_{C_3 D_1} + vr_{X_v D_1}$

2B. $r_{C_2 S_1} = cr_{D_2 S_1} + dr_{S_2 S_1} + ir_{C_2 S_1} + ir_{C_3 S_1}$

2C. $r_{C_2 D_2} = c + dr_{S_2 D_2} + ir_{C_1 D_2} + ir_{C_3 D_2}$

2D. $r_{C_2 S_2} = cr_{D_2 S_2} + d + ir_{C_1 S_2} + ir_{C_3 S_2}$

2E. $r_{C_2 D_3} = cr_{D_2 D_3} + dr_{S_2 D_3} + ir_{C_1 D_3} + ir_{C_3 D_3} + vr_{X_v D_3}$

2F. $r_{C_2 S_3} = cr_{D_2 S_3} + dr_{S_2 S_3} + ir_{C_1 S_3} + ir_{C_3 S_3} + vr_{X_v S_3}$

Here we require that the correlations of three predetermined variables with residuals are zero. However, we have only three unknowns, since i appears twice in each equation. As it turns out, though, we have only three independent equations in which all correlations are known, since Equations 2B and 2F are identical by our assumptions, and 2A and 2E (which are also identical) contain unknown correlations, leaving 2B, 2C, and 2D from which the parameters are estimated.

The parameter estimates themselves are not unreasonable. Although a and c are higher than would be expected on the basis of previous models, they both show strong negative effects of distance on contacts between F and R and B and R, the latter being weaker than the former. The direct effects of the contact variables on one another are negligible, a finding similar to that obtained in Chapter 5 (see Table 5.5). The similarity of findings is striking when one considers the differences in the models, the methods of estimation, and the difference in samples. It is particularly important that the introduction of distance and contact variables between father and brother does not explain the positive correlations among the other contact variables: factors other than the direct effects of contact variables on one another are still required to explain them.

It is impossible to unstandardize all of the coefficients, since we do not know the mean or standard deviation of C_3. It is also impossible to estimate the paths u and v, r_{uv}, and r_{uw}, since $r_{C_3C_1}$ is unknown. I did, however, make one test of the model's adequacy by using the coefficients previously estimated to solve either Equation 1A or Equation 2A for $r_{C_3D_1}$, by temporarily assuming the residual correlations in these equations to equal zero. Unfortunately, the correlations estimated by using either of these equations turn out to be greater than 1.0. Specifically, if we solve Equation 1A for $r_{C_3D_1}$ we obtain a value of 1.3657, and if we solve Equation 2A we find that $r_{C_3D_1} = 1.5954$. This result might call into question the validity of the whole model, and indeed this model is only a very tentative construction, not to be thought of as final in any sense. Before considering it completely inadequate, however, one should consider that the estimated correlations mentioned above are only estimates for the sample, not the population. They are, therefore, subject to sampling error which could make them fluctuate considerably. Furthermore, I assumed that the residual correlation in either Equation 1A or 2A equals zero in order to solve for $r_{C_3D_1}$.

In obtaining this correlation I find that a very small quantity is in the denominator of the expression (either g = .0268 or i = .0131). Using Equation 1A (and temporarily ignoring the term $ur_{X_uD_1}$), I found that $r_{C_3D_1} = \dfrac{.0366}{.0268}$. Thus a change of .01 in the numerator could yield a reasonable estimate of $r_{C_3D_1}$, rather than the impossible one obtained. This small amount could easily be accounted for by the correlation $r_{X_uD_1}$, which was not required to equal zero.

Thus it is quite possible that a small residual correlation of X_u and D_1 could change the numerator sufficiently to make the estimated correlation plausible. In any case, despite its flaws and incompleteness, this model does corroborate the findings of the earlier model, and it provides an example of the kind of model which might be used to describe the interdependence among three or more members of a kinship network.

COMPARISON OF LINEAR TO PROPORTIONAL MODEL FOR ESTIMATING THE RELATIONSHIP BETWEEN DISTANCE AND CONTACT WITH HUSBAND'S FATHER

The regression equation for a linear model to estimate the relationship between residential distance and contact with husband's father is:

$$C_i = 96.465 - .040\, D_i$$

Using regression to estimate the parameters for the proportional model, and regressing the natural log of contact on the natural log of distance, gives the result:

$$\ln C_i = 4.482 - .566 \ln D_i$$

One way to compare the two models is to compare the amounts of variation explained by them. For the linear model, $R^2 = .079$, indicating that the model explains about 8 percent of the variance in contact. For the proportional model, the R^2 estimated by regression is .626, approximately 63 percent. However, this comparison is misleading, for the R^2 for the proportional model tells what percentage of the variation in the *log* of contacts is explained by the log of distance. One way to make the R^2's comparable is to compute the antilogs of the expected values of log_e contact and use these values to obtain the correlation between expected and actual contact frequencies (see Goldberger, 1964:217). In doing so, I find that the proportion of variance in actual contact (rather than log_e contact) explained by the log model is .290, or about 29 percent, a figure still much larger than the 8 percent explained by the linear model.

Another way of comparing the models is to examine the goodness of fit of predicted values of parental contact at different points in the range of distance by comparing them to the observed mean frequencies of contact in those ranges.

If the model is appropriate, then each observed mean should be close to the predicted value of the mean of the appropriate distance category, and the mean of the residuals should be approximately zero regardless of the distance (or expected value of contact) involved. But Table F.1 demonstrates that these assumptions are not met in the linear model. (The distance ranges given in Table F.1 were chosen to coincide with equal-sized intervals on a logarithmic scale, on the assumption that the proportional model was more appropriate than the linear.)

TABLE F.1

Observed Mean Distance, Observed Mean Contact Frequency(Husband's Father), Predicted Contact Frequency, and Mean of Residuals for Specified Distance Categories. Predictions Made from Linear Model.

Distance Range	Observed Mean D	Observed Mean C	Predicted C at Mean D	Mean of Residuals	N
1 (Same City)	1.00	146.47	96.425	50.048	188
204 Miles	2.88	114.00	96.350	17.651	8
5-12 Miles	9.00	142.45	96.165	46.352	22
13-33 Miles	23.13	33.39	95.540	-62.145	31
34-90 Miles	58.20	20.82	94.137	-73.293	34
91-244 Miles	175.14	6.23	89.459	-83.166	28
245-665 Miles	385.67	3.56	81.038	-77.616	33
666-1810 Miles	1194.71	2.74	47.788	-45.522	42
1811-6800 Miles	3052.87	1.13	-25.650	28.240	23

Notation: D=Distance; C=Contact

Whereas the observed mean frequencies of contact decline rapidly with increasing distance, the predicted values do not do so until the very end of the distance range. The values predicted through most of the range are therefore unrealistic. Furthermore, the model predicts negative values for contact at large distances, and negative values are impossible, given the nature of the variable. These negative predictions account for the positive residuals at the longest distances, since a positive observed value minus a negative predicted value will give a larger positive value. Part of the positive trend (or decreasing negative trend) in the categories of longer distance is also due to the truncation caused by coding all values less than or equal to one as one. This sets an arbitrary lower limit on observed values and artificially raises the means of the residuals in categories with large numbers of these values.

Comparable observed means and predicted values are given of the proportional model in Table F.2. (The values have been left in logarithmic form rather than being converted to their antilogs.) Being interested in testing the assumption that the magnitude of the residuals is constant regardless of differences in distance, I wish to compare the size of the mean of residuals in the various distance ranges. Such comparisons, if made between the antilogs of the residuals, would be misleading if the proportional model is the correct one. The fact that the errors are multiplicative rather than additive in the proportional model means that the magnitude of the difference between residuals at different distances will vary with the distance. In this case the logarithmic residuals will provide the proper comparison, since the difference between the size of the logarithmic residuals will be constant, regardless of distance. Comparisons between residuals at different distances in a linear model are comparisons of additive differences. In order to compare additive differences in the residuals for a model in which the errors are actually multiplicative, the logarithmic errors must be compared.

TABLE F.2

Observed Mean Ln Distance, Observed Mean Ln Contact Frequency
(Husband's Father), Predicted Ln Contact Frequency, and Mean
of Ln Residuals for Specified Ln Distance Categories.
Predictions Made from Proportional Model.

Ln Distance Range	Observed Mean Ln D	Observed Mean Ln C	Predicted Ln C at Mean Ln D	Mean of Ln Residuals	N
0.0 (Same City)	0.000	4.355	4.482	−.127	188
0.50-1.49 Ln Miles	1.033	3.057	3.897	.148	8
1.50-2.49 Ln Miles	2.165	4.516	3.257	1.260	22
2.50-3.49 Ln Miles	3.102	3.035	2.726	.310	31
3.50-4.49 Ln Miles	4.023	2.373	2.205	.169	34
4.50-5.49 Ln Miles	5.128	1.456	1.580	−.122	28
5.50-6.49 Ln Miles	5.918	.725	1.132	−.475	33
6.50-7.49 Ln Miles	7.047	.358	.493	−.139	42
7.50-8.82 Ln Miles	7.948	.080	−.016	.198	23

Notation: Ln D= Log_e Distance; Ln C= Log_e Contact

Table 1.4 shows a slight irregularity in the observed mean ln contact frequencies, since·the frequency in the 1.50-2.49 ln mile distance range (equivalent to 4.5-12.1 miles) is larger than it is in the two preceding categories. This indication of nonmonotonicity is, I suspect, a consequence of the coding of all respondents in the same city as being one mile from parents (or as zero in the log scale), rather than of a defect in the model. It may also be that the mean for the second category (0.50-1.49 ln miles) is misleadingly low, since it is based on only eight respondents. If so, then the reversal is much smaller in magnitude than it at first appears.

In any case, the observed means and the predicted values correspond very closely. Although the predicted value of contact frequency at the longest distance range is negative, this is a legitimate prediction, since the logs of values between zero and one are negative, the antilog of −.016 being approximately .984 contacts per year. This seems reasonable for a distance range which is equivalent to 1791-6800 miles. Table F.2 also shows that the means of the log residuals are very close to zero and exhibit no systematic, or at least no monotonic tendency, to vary with distance. Here again the remarks about the truncation of observed values in the longest categories of distance apply. If the observed values were allowed to go below one, the mean residuals in the larger distance categories would not be artificially raised.

In summary, the proportional model is clearly superior to the linear, in terms both of explained variance and of the correspondence between observed values and those predicted by the model.

BIBLIOGRAPHY

Adams, Bert N.
  1968   Kinship in an Urban Setting. Chicago: Markham.
Aiken, Michael T.
  1964   Kinship in an Urban Community. Unpublished Doctoral Dissertation,
         Department of Sociology, University of Michigan.
Aiken, Michael T. and David Goldberg.
  1969   "Social Mobility and Kinship: A Re-examination of the Hypothesis."
         American Anthropologist, 71 (April), pp. 261-270.
Aitchison, J. and J. A. C. Brown.
  1957   The Lognormal Distribution. Cambridge: Cambridge University
         Press.
Aldous, Joan.
  1962   "Urbanization, the Extended Family, and Kinship Ties in West Af-
         rica." Social Forces, 41 (October), pp. 6-12.
Axelrod, Morris.
  1956   "Urban Structure and Social Participation." American Sociological
         Review, 21 (February), pp. 13-18.
Ayoub, Millicent R.
  1966   "The Family Reunion." Ethnology, 5 (October), pp. 415-448.
Bell, Wendell and Marion D. Boat.
  1957   "Urban Neighborhoods and Informal Social Relations." American
         Journal of Sociology, 62 (January), pp. 391-398.
Blau, Peter M.
  1956   "Social Mobility and Interpersonal Relations." American Sociological
         Review, 21 (June), pp. 290-295.
Blau, Peter M. and Otis Dudley Duncan.
  1967   The American Occupational Structure. New York: John Wiley.
Blumberg, Leonard and Robert R. Bell.
  1959   "Urban Migration and Kinship Ties." Social Problems, 6 (Spring),
         pp. 328-333.
Bossard, James H. S.
  1932   "Residential Propinquity as a Factor in Marriage Selection." Ameri-
         can Journal of Sociology, 38 (September), pp. 219-224.
Bossard, James H. S. and Eleanor S. Boll.
  1946   "The Immediate Family and the Kinship Group: A Research Report."
         Social Forces, 24 (March), pp. 379-384.
Bott, Elizabeth.
  1957   Kinship and Social Network. London: Tavistock Publications, Ltd.
Brav, Stanley R.
  1940   Jewish Family Solidarity—Myth or Fact? Vicksburg, Mississippi: No-
         gales Press.
Burgess, Ernest W.
  1960   "Family Structure and Relationships." In Ernest W. Burgess (ed.),
         Aging in Western Societies. Chicago: The University of Chicago
         Press, pp. 271-298.

Campisi, Paul J.
1948   "Ethnic Family Patterns: The Italian Family in the United States."
American Journal of Sociology, 53 (May), pp. 443-449.
Cavan, Ruth Shonle.
1948   "Regional Family Patterns: The Middle Western Family." American
Journal of Sociology, 53 (May), pp. 430-431.
Cavan, Ruth Shonle.
1949   "Family Life and Family Substitutes in Old Age." American Sociological Review, 14 (February), pp. 71-83.
Child, Irvin L.
1943   Italian or American? The Second Generation in Conflict. New Haven:
Yale University Press.
Codere, Helen.
1955   "A Genealogical Study of Kinship in the United States." Psychiatry,
18 (February), pp. 65-79.
Cumming, Elaine and David M. Schneider.
1961   "Sibling Solidarity: A Property of American Kinship." American Anthropologist, 63 (June), pp. 498-507.
Duncan, Otis Dudley.
1957   "Community Size and the Urban-Rural Continuum." In Paul K. Hatt
and Albert J. Reiss, Jr. (eds.), Cities and Society. New York: The Free
Press, pp. 35-45.
Duncan, Otis Dudley.
1966   "Path Analysis: Sociological Examples." American Journal of Sociology, 72 (July), pp. 1-16.
Duncan, Otis Dudley.
1969   "Some Linear Models for Two-Wave, Two Variable Panel Analysis."
Psychological Bulletin, 72, pp. 177-182.
Duncan, Otis Dudley.
1970   "Duncan's Corrections of Published Text of 'Peer Influences on Aspi-
rations: A Reinterpretation'." American Journal of Sociology, 75
(May), pp. 1042-1046.
Duncan, Otis Dudley and Leo F. Schnore.
1959   "Cultural, Behavioral, and Ecological Perspectives in the Study of Social Organization." American Journal of Sociology, 65 (September),
pp. 132-146.
Duncan, Otis Dudley, Archibald O. Haller and Alejandro Portes.
1968   "Peer Influences on Aspiration: A Reinterpretation." American Journal of Sociology, 74 (September), pp. 119-137.
Farber, Bernard.
1968   Comparative Kinship Systems. New York: John Wiley.
Firth, Raymond.
1964   "Family and Kinship in Industrial Society." In Paul Halmos (ed.),
The Sociological Review Monograph No. 8: The Development of Industrial Societies. Keele: University of Keele, pp. 65-87.
Firth, Raymond and Judith Djamour.
1956   "Kinship in South Borough." In Raymond Firth (ed.), Two Studies of
Kinship in London. London: The Athlone Press, pp. 33-46.

Firth, Raymond, Jane Hubert and Anthony Forge.
  1969   Families and Their Relatives. London: Routledge and Kegan Paul.
Firey, Walter.
  1947   Land Use in Central Boston. Cambridge, Massachusetts: Harvard University Press.
Folsom, Joseph K.
  1948   "Regional Family Patterns: The New England Family." American Journal of Sociology, 53 (May), pp. 423-425.
Furstenberg, Frank F., Jr.
  1966   "Industrialization and the American Family: A Look Backward." American Sociological Review, 31 (June), pp. 326-337.
Gans, Herbert J.
  1962   The Urban Villagers. New York: The Free Press.
Garigue, Philip.
  1956   "French Canadian Kinship and Urban Life." American Anthropologist, 58 (December), pp. 1090-1101.
Garigue, Philip and Raymond Firth.
  1956   "Kinship Organization of Italianates in London." In Raymond Firth (ed.), Two Studies of Kinship in London. University of London: The Athlone Press, pp. 67-93.
Glazer, Nathan and Daniel Patrick Moynihan.
  1963   Beyond the Melting Pot. Cambridge, Massachusetts: Massachusetts Institute of Technology Press.
Gockel, Galen L.
  1969   "Income and Religious Affiliation: A Regression Analysis." American Journal of Sociology, 74 (May), pp. 632-647.
Goldberger, Arthur S.
  1964   Econometric Theory. New York: John Wiley and Sons.
Goldstein, Sidney.
  1969   "Socioeconomic Differentials Among Religious Groups in the United States." American Journal of Sociology, 74 (May), pp. 612-631.
Goode, Erich.
  1966   "Social Class and Church Participation." American Journal of Sociology, 72 (July), pp. 102-111.
Greenfield, Sidney M.
  1961   "Industrialization and the Family in Sociological Theory." American Journal of Sociology, 67 (November), pp. 312-322.
Hayner, Norman S.
  1948   "Regional Family Patterns: The Western Family." American Journal of Sociology, 53 (May), pp. 432-434.
Herberg, Will.
  1960   Protestant-Catholic-Jew. Garden City, New York: Doubleday Anchor, rev. ed.
Hill, T. P.
  1959   "An Analysis of the Distribution of Wages and Salaries in Great Britain." Econometrica, 27 (July), pp. 355-381.
Humphrey, Norman D.
  1944   "The Changing Structure of the Detroit Mexican Family: An Index of

Acculturation." American Sociological Review, 9 (December), pp. 622-626.

Hollingshead, August B. and Frederick C. Redlich.
1958 Social Class and Mental Illness. New York: John Wiley and Sons, Inc.

Irish, Donald P.
1964 "Sibling Interaction: A Neglected Aspect in Family Life Research." Social Forces, 42 (March), pp. 279-288.

Janowitz, Morris.
1956 "Some Consequences of Social Mobility in the United States." Transactions of the Third World Congress of Sociology, International Sociological Association, 3, pp. 191-201.

Johnston, J.
1963 Econometric Methods. New York: McGraw-Hill.

Lansing, John B. and Leslie Kish.
1957 "Family Life Cycle as an Independent Variable." American Sociological Review, 25 (October), pp. 512-519.

Laumann, Edward O.
1969 "The Social Structure of Religious and Ethnoreligious Groups in a Metropolitan Community." American Sociological Review, 34 (April), pp. 182-197.

Lemasters, E. E.
1954 "Social Class Mobility and Family Integration." Marriage and Family Living, 16 (August), pp. 226-232.

Lenski, Gerhard.
1963 The Religious Factor. Garden City, New York: Doubleday, Anchor, rev. ed.

Litwak, Eugene.
1960 "Occupational Mobility and Extended Family Cohesion." American Sociological Review, 25 (February), pp. 9-21.

Litwak, Eugene.
1960 "Geographic Mobility and Extended Family Cohesion." American Sociological Review, 25 (June), pp. 385-394.

Litwak, Eugene and Ivan Szelenyi.
1969 "Primary Group Structures and Their Functions: Kin, Neighbors, and Friends." American Sociological Review, 34 (August), pp. 465-481.

Locke, Harvey J.
1940 "Mobility and Family Disorganization." American Sociological Review, 5 (August), pp. 489-494.

Loomis, Charles P.
1936 "The Study of the Life Cycle of Families." Rural Sociology, 1 (June), pp. 180-189.

Lopreato, Joseph.
1970 Italian Americans. New York: Random House.

Loudon, J. B.
1961 "Kinship and Crisis in South Wales." British Journal of Sociology, 12 (December), pp. 333-350.

Melichar, Emanuel.
1965 "Least Squares Analysis of Economic Survey Data." Proceedings of

the Business and Economics Section of the American Statistical Association.

Michel, Andrée Vielle.
1960 "Kinship Relations and Relationships of Proximity in French Working-Class Households." In Norman W. Bell and Ezra F. Vogel (eds.), A Modern Introduction to the Family. Glencoe: The Free Press, pp. 287-294.

Michelson, William.
1971 "Some Like It Hot: Social Participation and Environmental Use as Functions of the Season." American Journal of Sociology, 76 (May), pp. 1072-1083.

Mitchell, William E.
1961 "Descent Groups Among New York City Jews." Jewish Journal of Sociology, pp. 121-128.

Mogey, J. M.
1956 Family and Neighborhood. Oxford: Oxford University Press.

Molotch, Harvey.
1969 "Racial Integration in a Transition Community." American Sociological Review, 34 (December), pp. 878-893.

Moynihan, Daniel P. (ed.)
1969 On Understanding Poverty. New York: Basic Books.

Munch, Peter A.
1949 "Social Adjustment Among Wisconsin Norwegians." American Sociological Review, 14 (December), pp. 780-787.

Ogburn, William Fielding and Otis Dudley Duncan.
1964 "City Size as a Sociological Variable." In Ernest W. Burgess and Donald J. Bogue (eds.), Contributions to Urban Sociology. Chicago: University of Chicago Press, pp. 129-147.

Parsons, Talcott.
1954 "The Kinship System of the Contemporary United States." In Essays in Sociological Theory, revised. New York: Free Press, pp. 177-196.

Reiss, Paul J.
1962 "The Extended Kinship System: Correlates of and Attitudes on Frequency of Interaction." Marriage and Family Living, 24 (November), pp. 333-339.

Robins, Lee N. and Miroda Tomanec.
1962 "Closeness to Blood Relatives Outside the Immediate Family." Marriage and Family Living, 24 (November), pp. 340-346.

Rosenmayr, Leopold.
1968 "Family Relations of the Elderly." Journal of Marriage and the Family, 30 (November), pp. 672-680.

Rosett, Richard N.
1959 "A Statistical Model of Friction in Economics." Econometrica, 27, pp. 263-267.

Samuelson, Paul A.
1958 Economics: An Introductory Analysis. 4th ed. New York: McGraw-Hill.

Schneider, David M.
1968 American Kinship. Englewood Cliffs, New Jersey: Prentice-Hall.

Schneider, David M. and George C. Homans
 1955   "Kinship Terminology and the American Kinship System." American
        Anthropologist, 57 (December), pp. 1194-1208.
Sharp, Harry and Morris Axelrod.
 1956   "Mutual Aid Among Relatives in an Urban Population." In Ronald
        Freedman, et al. (eds.), Principles of Sociology, revised. New York:
        Holt, Rinehart, and Winston, pp. 433-439.
Shaw, Lulie A.
 1954   "Impressions of Family Life in a London Suburb." Sociological Re-
        view, new series, 2 (December), pp. 179-194.
Smelser, Neil J. and S. M. Lipset (eds.)
 1966   Social Structure and Mobility in Economic Development. Chicago:
        Aldine.
Strodtbeck, Fred L.
 1958   "Family Interaction, Values and Achievement." In David C. McClel-
        land, et al., Talent and Society. Princeton, New Jersey: D. Van Nos-
        trand, pp. 135-194.
Stuckert, Robert P.
 1963   "Occupational Mobility and Family Relationships." Social Forces, 41
        (March), pp. 301-307.
Sudman, Seymour
 1966   "Probability Sampling with Quotas," Journal of the American Statis-
        tical Association, 61 (September), pp. 749-771.
Suits, Daniel B.
 1957   "The Use of Dummy Variables in Regression Equations." Journal of
        the American Statistical Association, 52 (December), pp. 548-555.
Sussman, Marvin B.
 1959   "The Isolated Nuclear Family: Fact or Fiction." Social Problems, 6
        (Spring), pp. 333-340.
Sussman, Marvin B. and Lee Burchinal.
 1962   "Kin Family Network: Unheralded Structure in Current Conceptuali-
        zations of Family Functioning." Marriage and Family Living, 24 (Au-
        gust), pp. 231-240.
Sussman, Marvin B. and R. Clyde White.
 1959   Hough, Cleveland, Ohio: A Study of Social Life and Change. Cleve-
        land: The Press of Western Reserve University.
Thomas, John L.
 1956   The American Catholic Family. Englewood Cliffs, New Jersey: Pren-
        tice-Hall.
Tobin, J.
 1958   "Estimation of Relationships for Limited Dependent Variables."
        Econometrica, 26 (January), pp. 24-36.
Toennies, Ferdinand.
 1961   "Gemeinschaft and Gesellschaft." In Talcott Parsons, et al., Theories
        of Society. New York: Free Press, pp. 191-201.
Townsend, Peter.
 1955   "The Family Life of Old People: An Investigation in East London."
        Sociological Review, new series, 3, pp. 175-195.

Vance, Rupert B.
1948 "Regional Family Patterns: The Southern Family." American Journal of Sociology, 53 (May), pp. 426-429.

Walker, Helen M. and Joseph Lev.
1953 Statistical Inference. New York: Henry Holt and Co.

Warner, W. Lloyd and Leo Srole.
1945 The Social Systems of American Ethnic Groups. New Haven, Connecticut: Yale University Press.

Wilensky, Harold L.
1961 "Life Cycle, Work Situation, and Participation in Formal Associations." In Robert W. Kleemeier (ed.), Aging and Leisure. New York: Oxford University Press, pp. 213-242.

Williamson, Robert C.
1962 "Some Variables of Middle and Lower Class in Two Central American Cities." Social Forces, 41 (December), pp. 195-207.

Willmott, Peter and Michael Young.
1960 Family and Class in a London Suburb. London: Routledge and Kegan Paul.

Wilson, Bryan.
1968 "Religion and the Churches in Contemporary America." In William William G. McLoughlin and Robert N. Bellah (eds.), Religion in America. Boston: Houghton Mifflin, pp. 73-110.

Winch, Robert F., Scott Greer and Rae Lesser Blumberg.
1967 "Ethnicity and Extended Families in an Upper-Middle-Class Suburb." American Sociological Review, 32 (April), pp. 265-272.

Young, Michael and Peter Willmott.
1957 Family and Kinship in East London. Glencoe, Illinois: The Free Press.